I0755000

EVERYDAY WONDER

Sophie Howarth

The whole world is a series of miracles but we're so used to them we call them ordinary things.

— Hans Christian Andersen

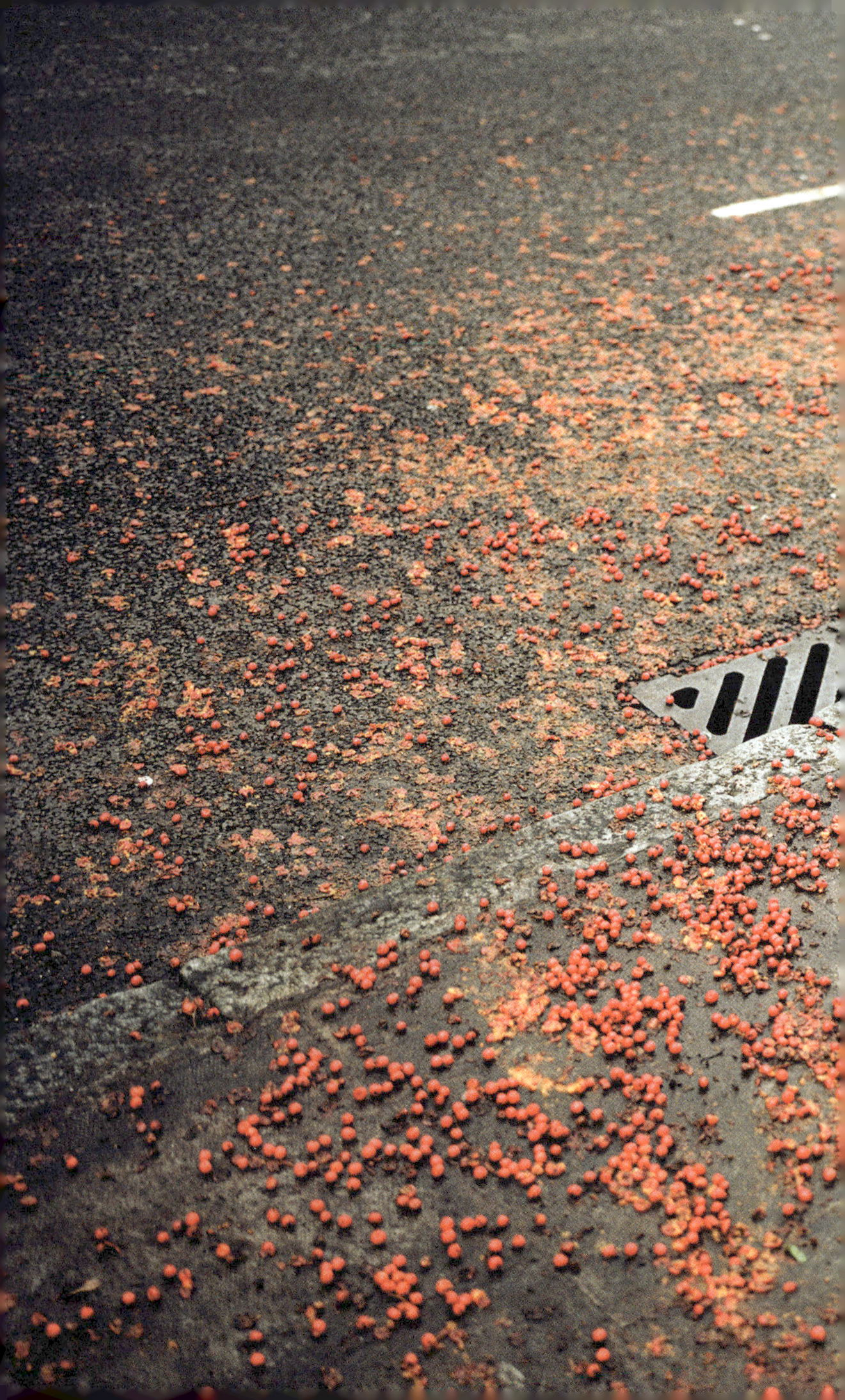

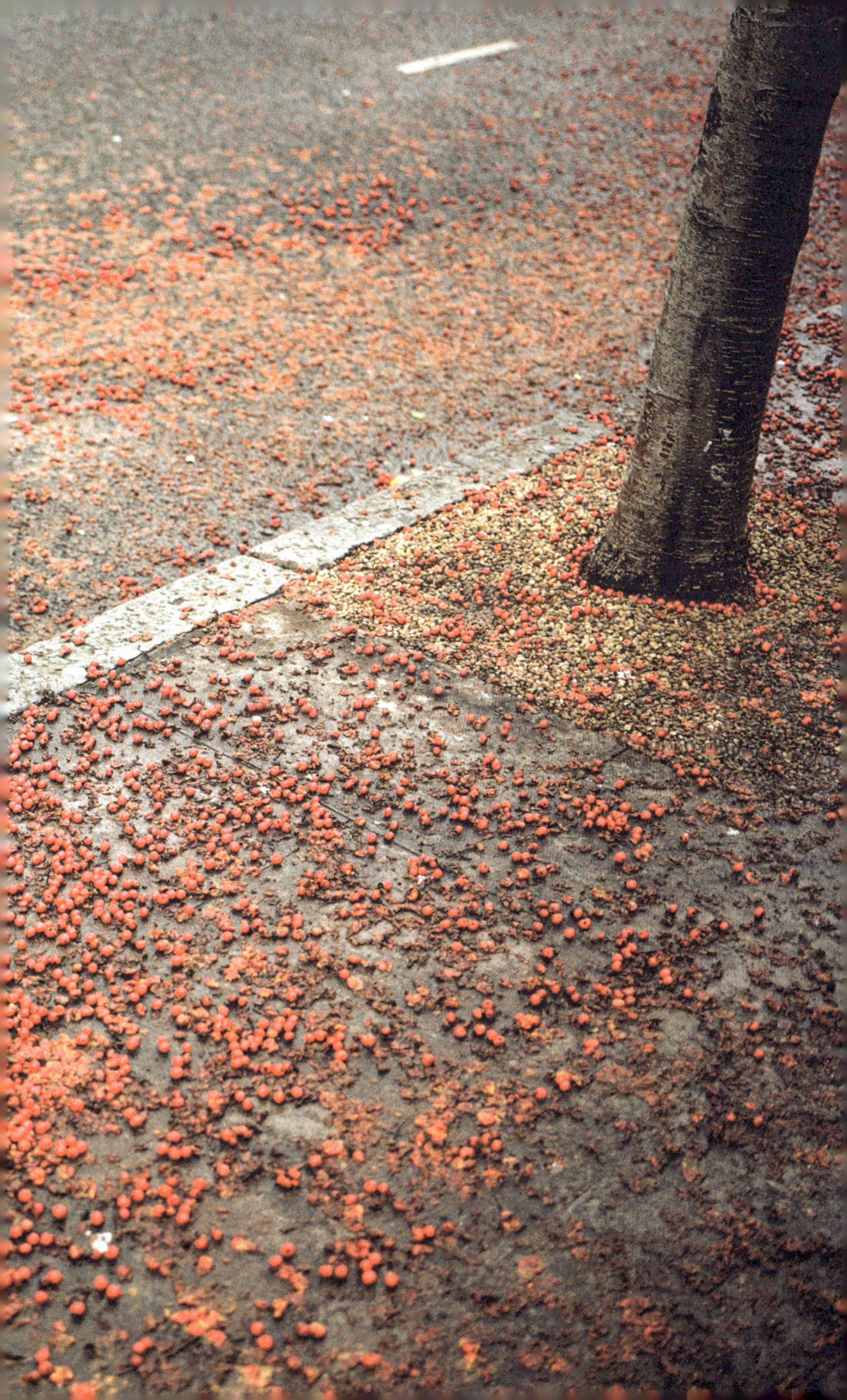

Previous: Zed Nelson, *Fallen Berries, Hackney*, 2013

YOU READING THIS, BE READY

Starting here, what do you want to remember?
How sunlight creeps along a shining floor?
What scent of old wood hovers, what softened
sound from outside fills the air?

Will you ever bring a better gift for the world
than the breathing respect that you carry
wherever you go right now? Are you waiting
for time to show you some better thoughts?

When you turn around, starting here, lift this
new glimpse that you found; carry into evening
all that you want from this day. This interval you spent
reading or hearing this, keep it for life –

What can anyone give you greater than now,
starting here, right in this room, when you turn around?

— *William Stafford*

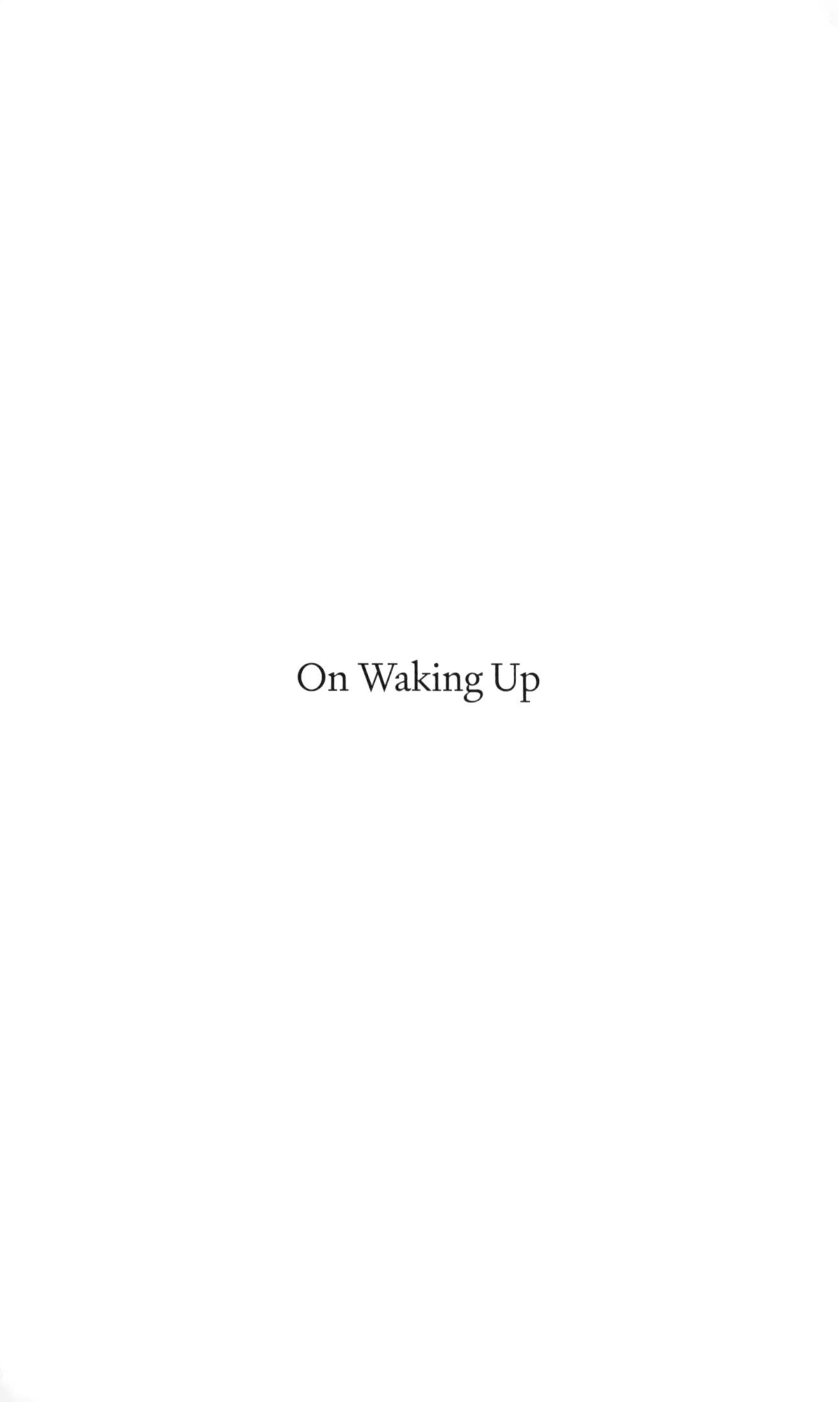

On Waking Up

This is a wonderful day. I've never seen this one before.

— tweet sent by poet Maya Angelou, aged 85

What would it be like to greet each day with wide-eyed curiosity? To get dressed, boil the kettle, travel to work and write your name as if for the first time? Astonishing, no doubt, but also highly impractical. To make it through daily life with some semblance of calm and competence, we humans have evolved to live much of our lives on autopilot, tuning out almost everything that's going on around us. As you read this paragraph, you're likely not thinking about your heart beating, your nerves firing or your gut digesting. You're probably not noticing the tiny creatures co-habiting the room you're in or the vast microbiome of bacteria, fungi and viruses in the air you're breathing. When you go outside, you might not pay much attention to the clouds shifting, the trees gurgling or the insects pollinating. A degree of oblivion is how we stay efficient with our most precious resource – our attention. But efficiency comes at a cost. There is a wonderland around, between and within us that we barely even notice.

This book is an invitation to resist narrowing our perceptual capacities and stretch our senses to take in a little more of the world we live in: to rub our tongues over our slippery, clean teeth after we've brushed them, to watch mesmerising soap patterns while we're washing up or to let ourselves become transfixed by a plastic bag fluttering in the wind as we wander down the street. These may not be activities our culture considers constructive, but we are not just here to be useful. Sometimes, the wildness of presence is more rewarding than the compliance of productivity.

It's a strange paradox that today, many of us have access to more wonders than ever before and yet so frequently find ourselves bored or disenchanted. At the swipe of a screen, we can watch a king penguin courting ritual on TikTok, take a virtual tour of Tutankhamun's tomb on YouTube or see the Northern Lights dancing on a webcam. Why do we so often feel indifferent?

Research suggests that our brains have begun to change in response to a faster, more fragmented world. We now find it harder to focus on – or appreciate – one thing deeply. We endlessly chase new tastes, new sights and new thrills, only to find that we have kicked our longings just a little further down the road. Many of us look to mindfulness apps to restore our sense of astonishment or repair our fractured attention spans, but often these too become lacklustre after just a few days. A hunger for real connection hovers in the air between a cacophony of wireless signals.

This book proposes that we call off the search for 'wondrous' things and consider how we might notice more of the beauty hiding in plain sight. Wonder, it turns out, is not an inherent quality of things in the world but an attitude of mind. Spiritual teachers tell us that accessing it is simple; we only need to bring our full attention. But that's easier said than done. In a world hellbent on distracting us, paying attention can feel like finding the Holy Grail. It's surprisingly hard to notice what's under our noses when we're busy checking our phones 50 times a day. Few of us doubt we'd be happier if we were more observant of, and grateful for, what's right in front of us, but many of us feel worn out by all the advice about how to do it.

Now that we live more and more of our lives second- or third-hand through the circulation of photos and videos, it's no surprise we often feel some of the freshness has worn off. Tethered to the screen, it's easy to lose confidence in our direct observations. But it's worth remembering that, once upon a time, we were all experts in exploring the world for ourselves. As babies, we touched, tasted, smelled, climbed over, poked, took apart, watched and listened to everything we encountered without preference or judgement. We delighted in touching our own and other people's bodies, eating whatever we could get our hands on, climbing into the lap of anyone we met. Curiosity was our chief characteristic, and every day was wonder-filled.

At some point in all our lives, well-meaning adults stepped in to teach us what was safe to touch and what was not, what was nice to smell and what was not, what was good to eat and what was not, what belonged to us and what did not. So it was that we came to see spiderwebs as beautiful but spiders as scary, water as life-giving but rain as irritating, people as kind but strangers as dangerous, bodies as marvellous though we should not admire our own too much. We were educated in the ways of the world, but we lost a good deal of our natural curiosity in the process.

'Sell your cleverness and buy bewilderment,' wrote the 13th-century Sufi poet Rumi. Bewilderment – what a word! It literally includes the instruction to *be wilder*. To shake off learned perceptions and hand-me-down interpretations and let the wild animal inside us be astonished by the smell, colour, form, shape, texture and taste of everything we encounter. I hope this book will assist you in recovering what the Buddhists call 'a beginner's mind', the disposition of openness and eagerness that returns magic to the mundane.

Across four chapters exploring Home, Street, Land and Body, we'll consider ways to peel back the film of familiarity and recover a sense of enchantment with what's immediately around us. Our guides on this journey are poets and photographers who marvel and delight in the things that many of us overlook: how the floor receives the bottom of our shoes, how the rain makes patterns on the window of the bus, how lovers wrap themselves around one another while sleeping at night. *Look!* They all say in their different ways. Look at the laundry hanging on the line, look at the glass spilled onto the pavement, look at this hair, look at these hands, look at this grapefruit, this potato, this sadness, this sweetness. All of it is astonishing.

At the end of each chapter, I've offered a few practices to deepen your sense of wonder. These are simple exercises you can do anytime and anywhere: alternatives to scrolling when you have a free moment. I make no promises of grand revelations, but I'm quietly hopeful they will help restore some of your childlike curiosity and delight. Above all, I hope they'll convince you there's no need to rush off anywhere in search of remarkable things. You are surrounded by – indeed, you are yourself a part of – an everyday wonderland.

Overleaf: Catherine Falls, 2021

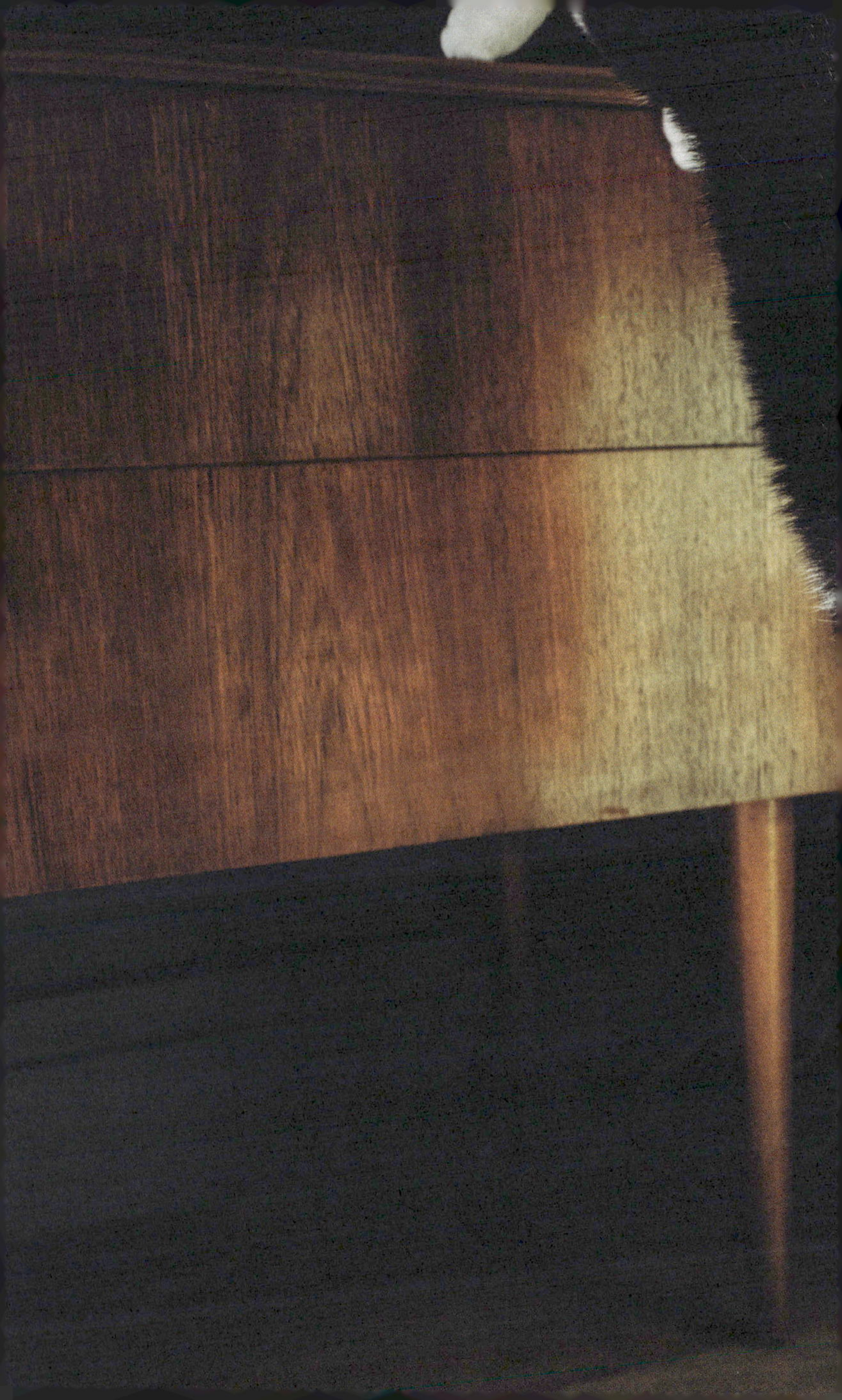

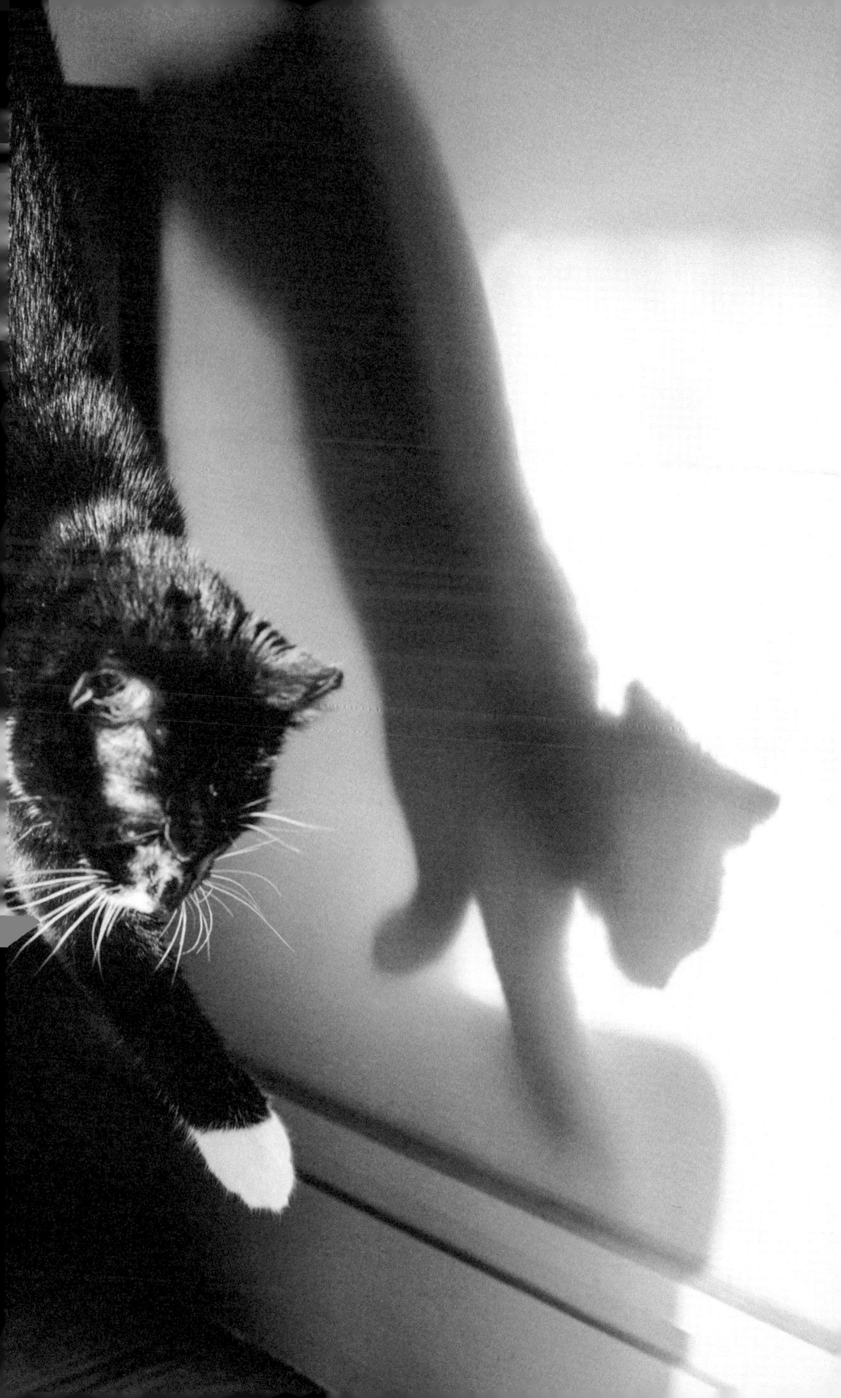

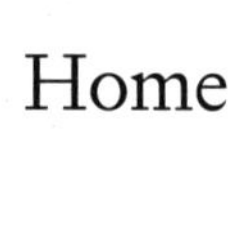
Home

Home is such an evocative word. It can describe a place and a feeling, a collection of rooms, a web of relationships, an accumulation of things or a mesh of memories. Often, the realities of home don't live up to the ideals we hold for it: we long for love, safety and belonging, and we end up arguing about whose turn it is to load the dishwasher or take the bins out.

The familiarity of home can make it a challenging place to find everyday wonder. The people, pets and things we live with day to day are hard to see with fresh eyes. But the poems and photographs collected here show that, hidden among the clutter of familiar objects and domestic duties, there are infinite daily opportunities for astonishment. Consider the origins of the fruit sitting in a bowl or the wood used to make the kitchen table. Watch the sunlight as it moves across the bedroom wall or catch the scent of garden plants alongside the drying laundry.

Our homes may often be messy, imperfect and stressful places, but they are also our daily temples, where making the bed or pouring the tea can become a quiet form of prayer. This chapter offers a gentle invitation to laugh at the list of undone jobs and reclaim the ordinary moments of tenderness and joy.

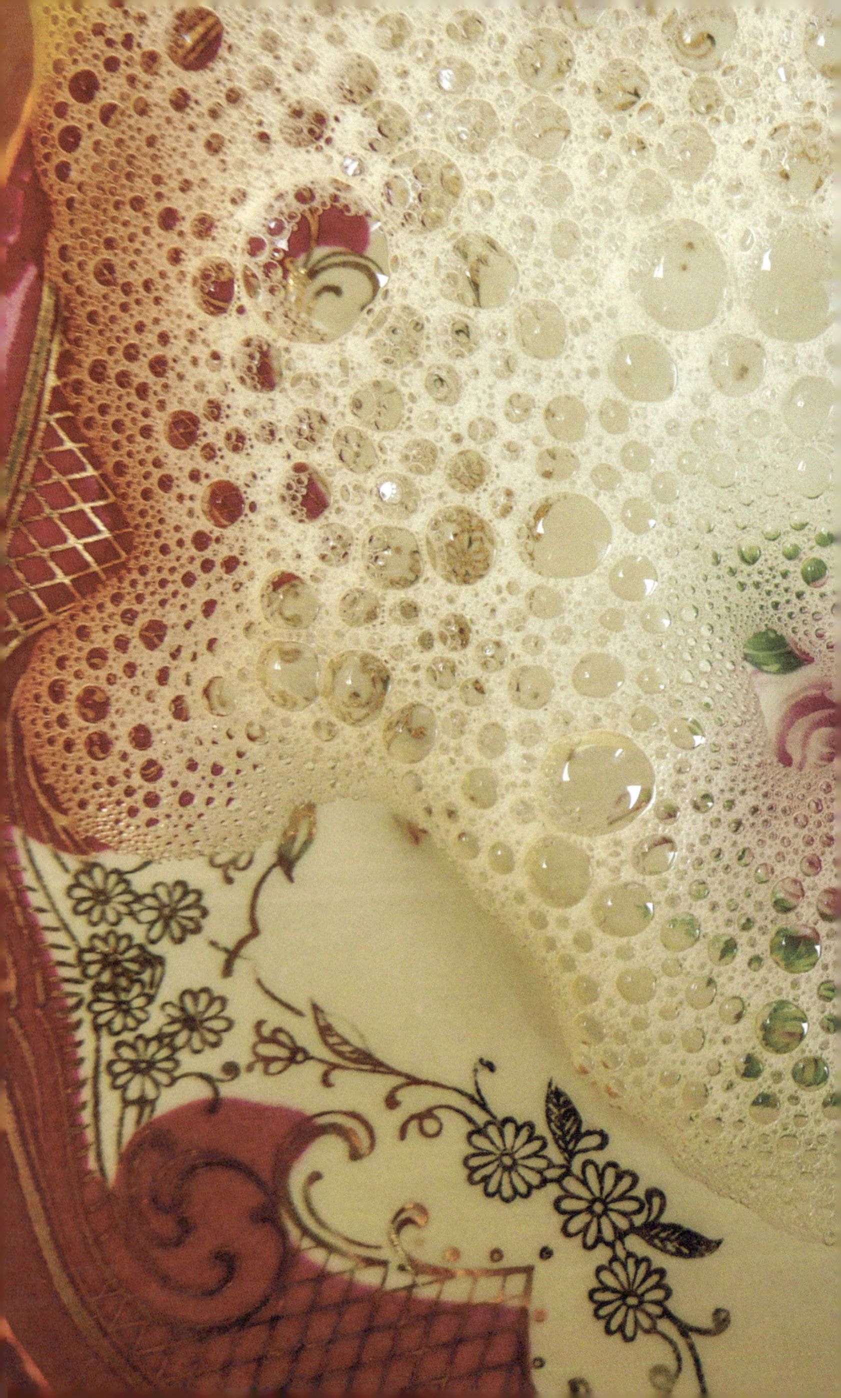

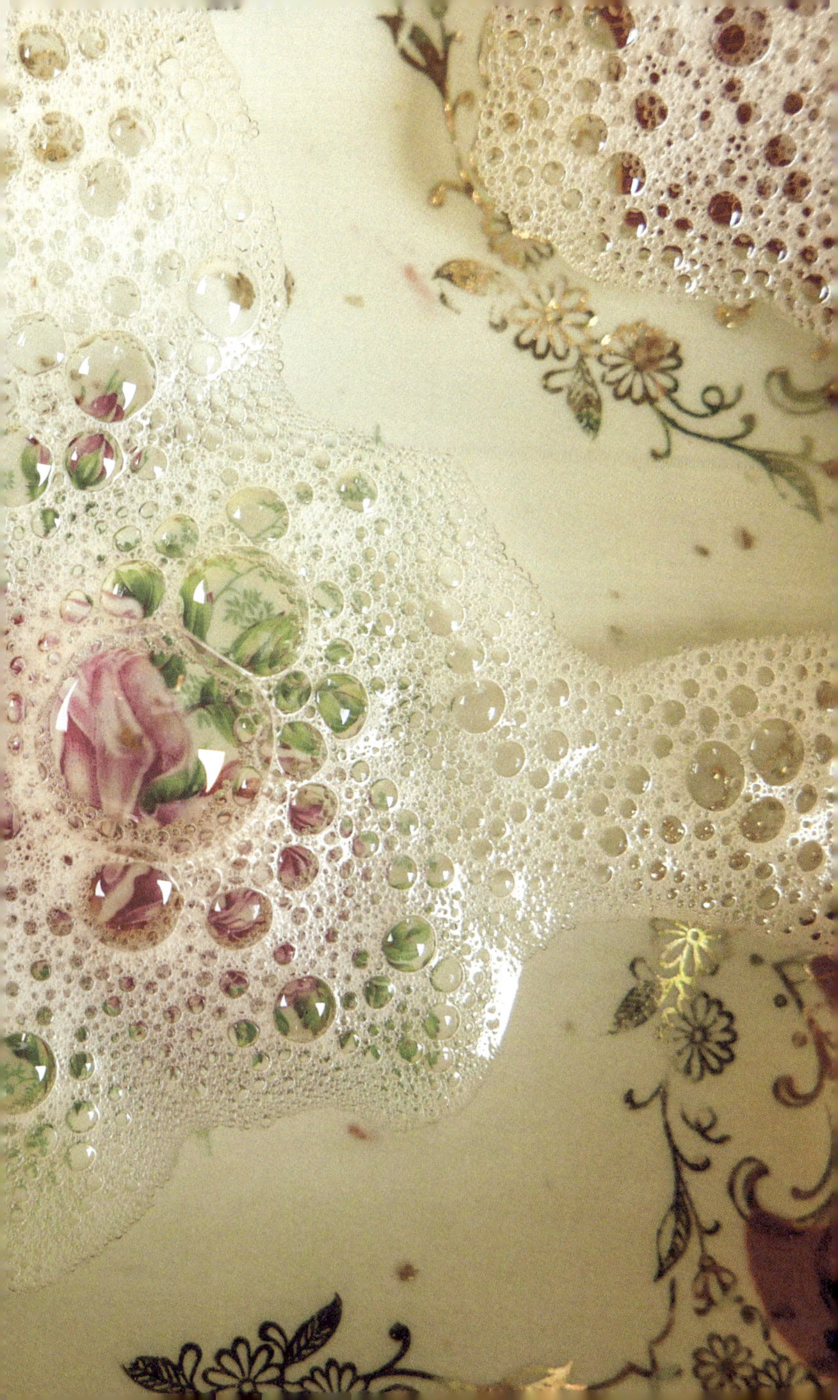

MEDITATION ON A GRAPEFRUIT

To wake when all is possible
before the agitations of the day
have gripped you
                              To come to the kitchen
and peel a little basketball
for breakfast
                    To tear the husk
like cotton padding   a cloud of oil
misting out of its pinprick pores
clean and sharp as pepper
                                        To ease
each pale pink section out of its case
so carefully   without breaking
a single pearly cell

Previous: Hiltrud Enders, *Washing Up*, 2023

To slide each piece
into a cold blue china bowl
the juice pooling until the whole
fruit is divided from its skin
and only then to eat
so sweet
a discipline
precisely pointless a devout
involvement of the hands and senses
a pause a little emptiness

each year harder to live within
each year harder to live without

— *Craig Arnold*

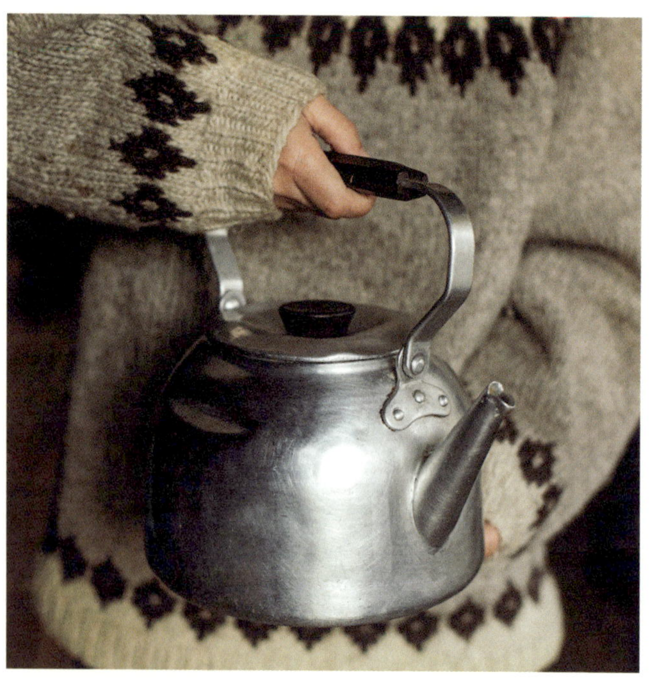

Miquel Llonch, 2016

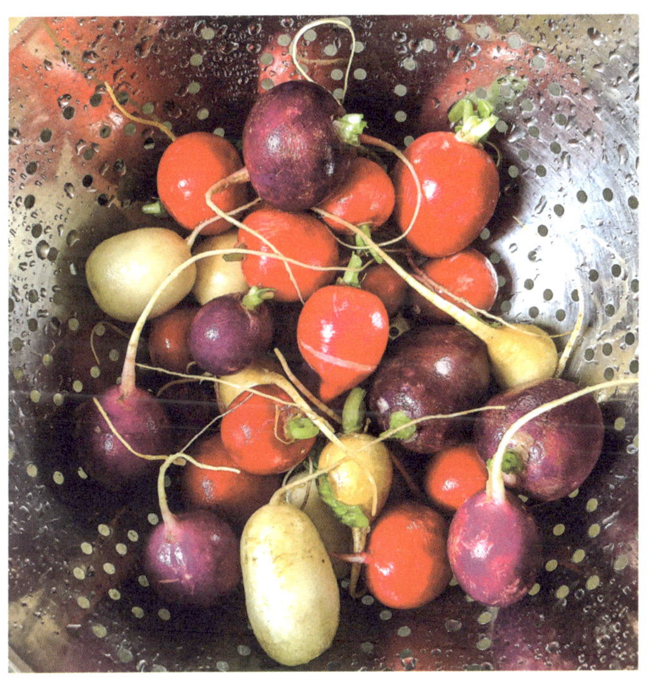

Johanna Neurath, 2020

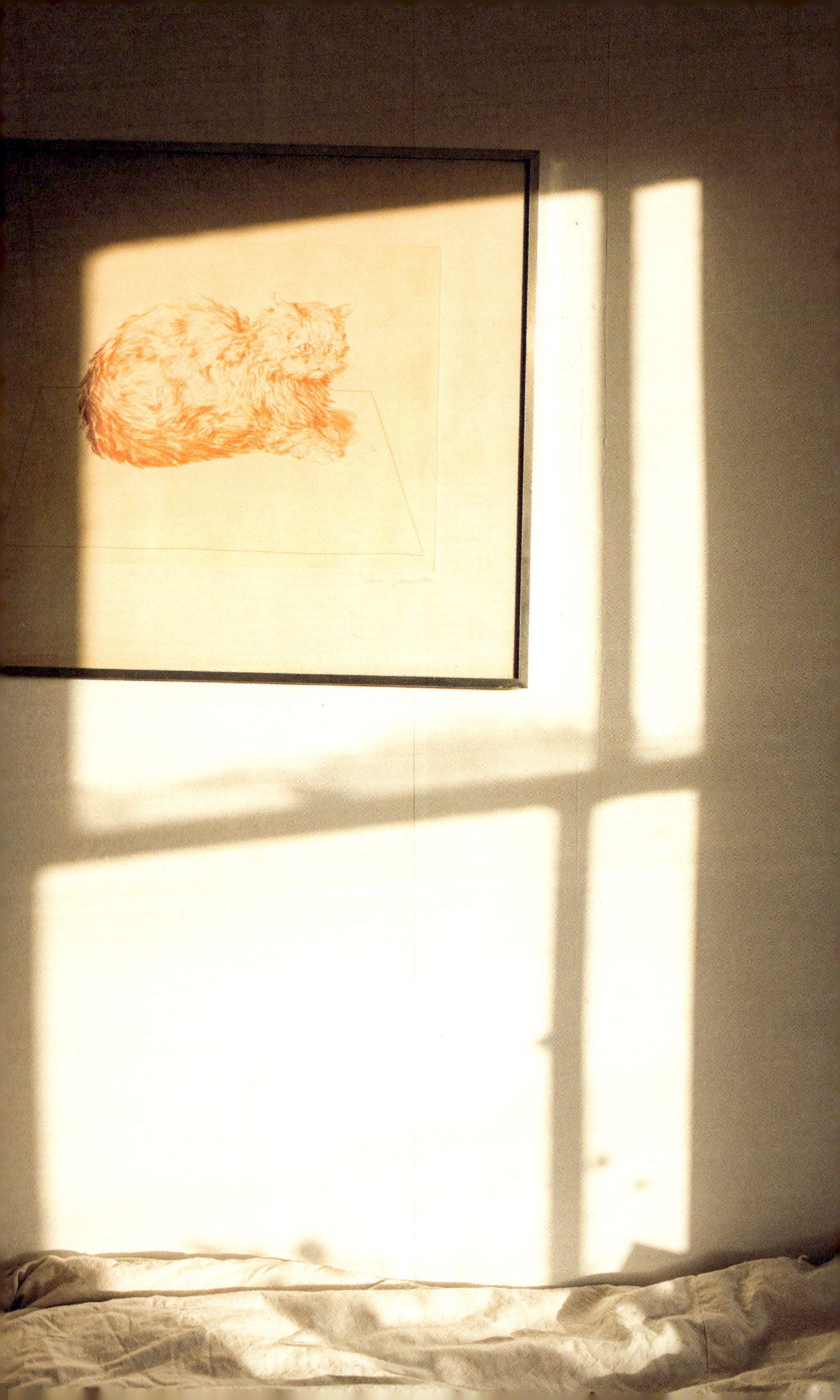

THE TEAPOT

That morning I heard water being poured into a teapot.
The sound was an ordinary, daily, cluffy sound.
But all at once, I knew you loved me.
An unheard-of-thing, love audible in water falling.

— *Robert Bly*

Left: Celine Marchbank, 2022

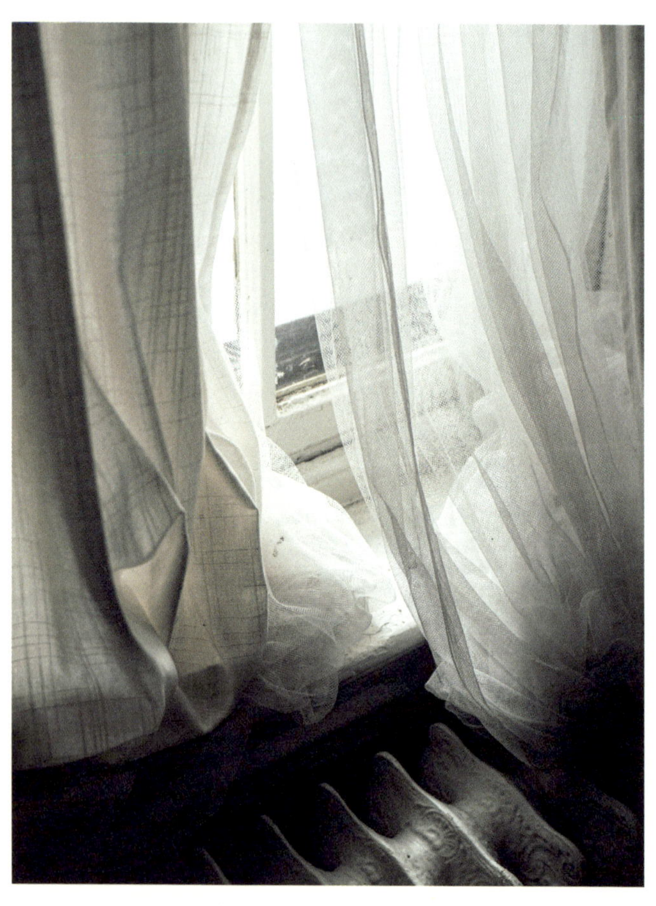

Nellie Adamyan, 2023

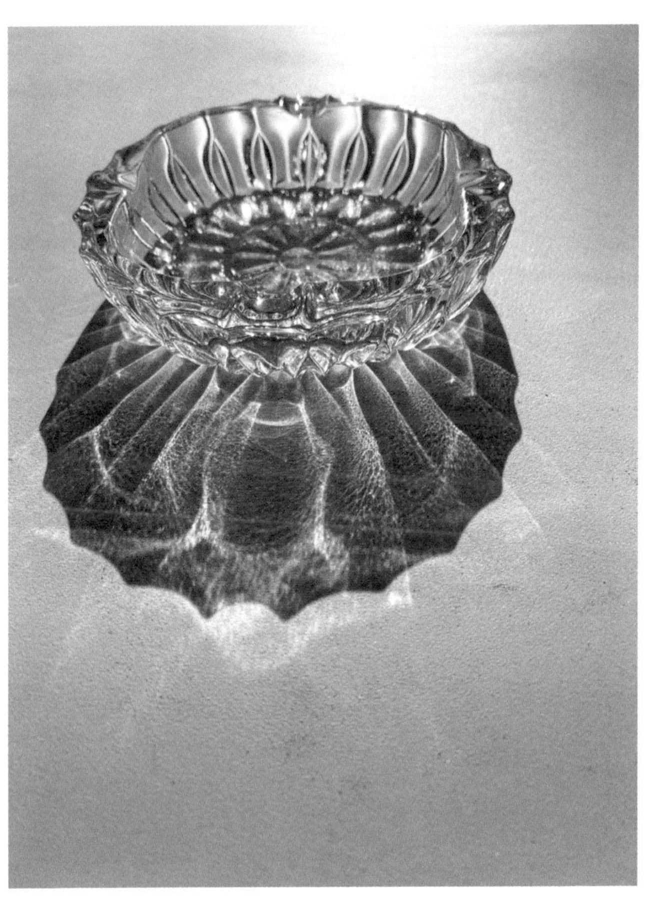

Jenny Lewis, *Solace*, 2024

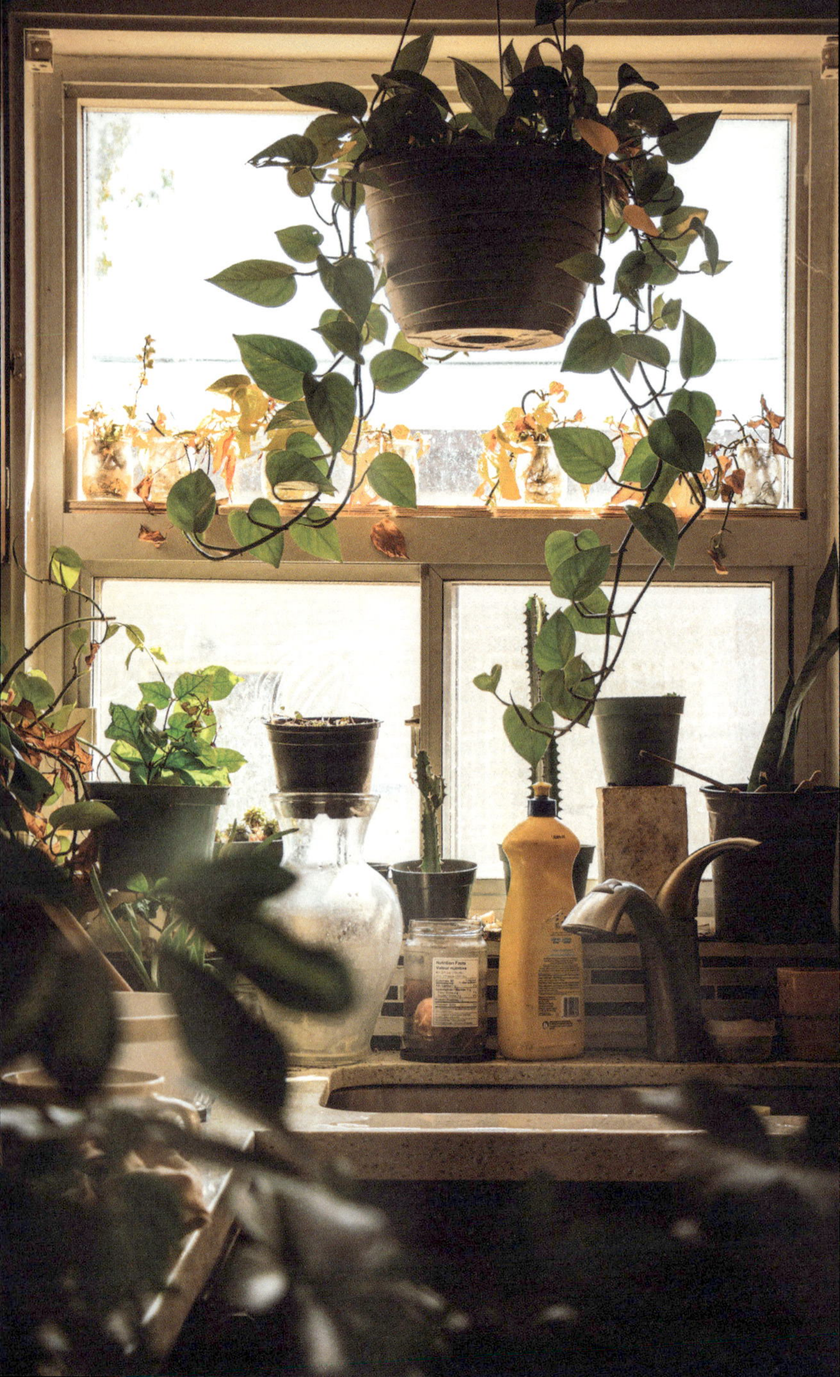

ODE

Here's to everything undone today:
laundry left damp in the machine,
the relatives unrung, the kitchen
drawer not sorted; here's to jeans
unpatched and buttons missing,
the dirty dishes, the novel
not yet started. To Christmas
cards unsent in March, to emails
marked unread. To friends unmet
and deadlines unaddressed;
to every item not crossed off the list;
to everything still left, ignored, put off:
it is enough.

— *Zoe Higgins*

Left: Lianhao Qu, 2020

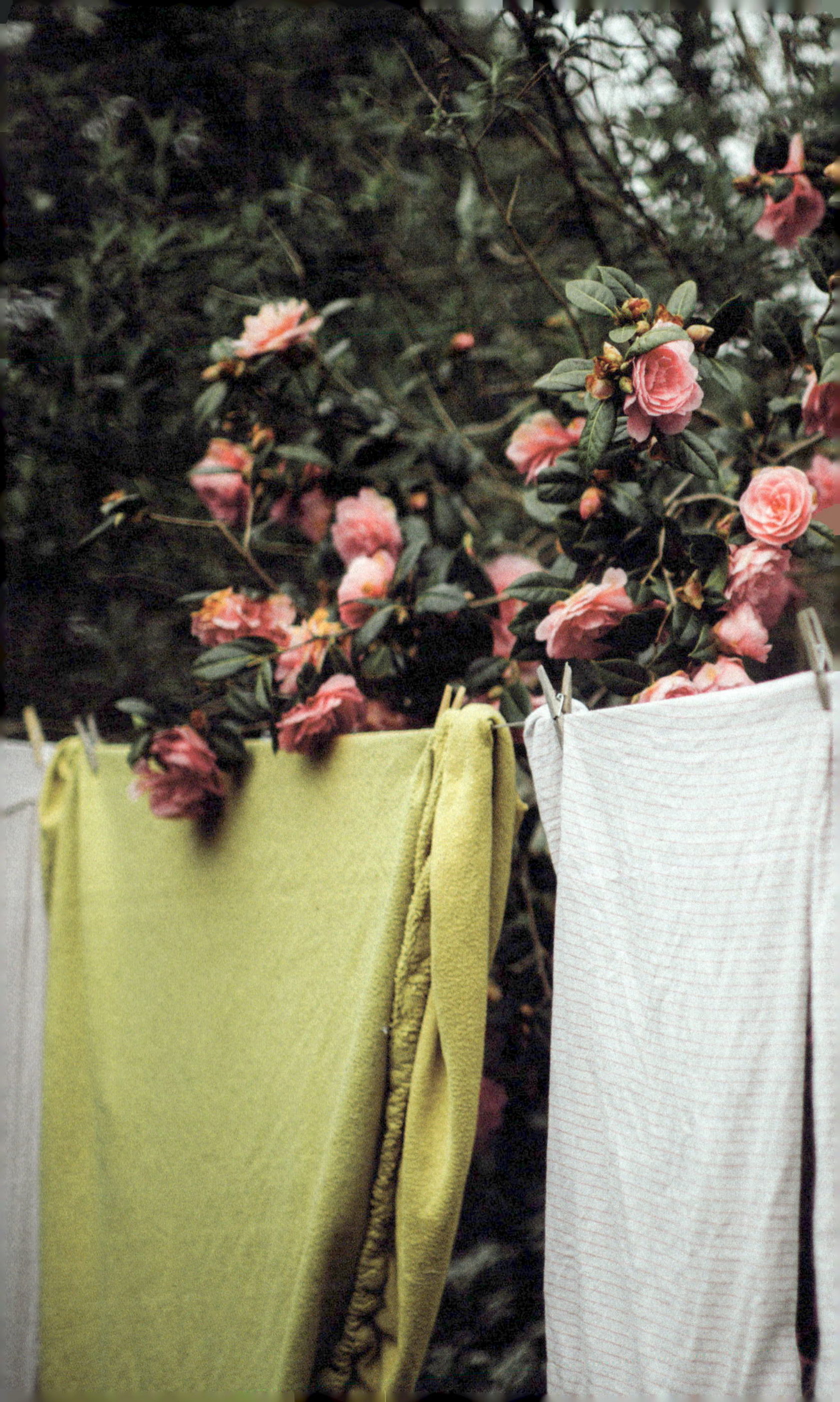

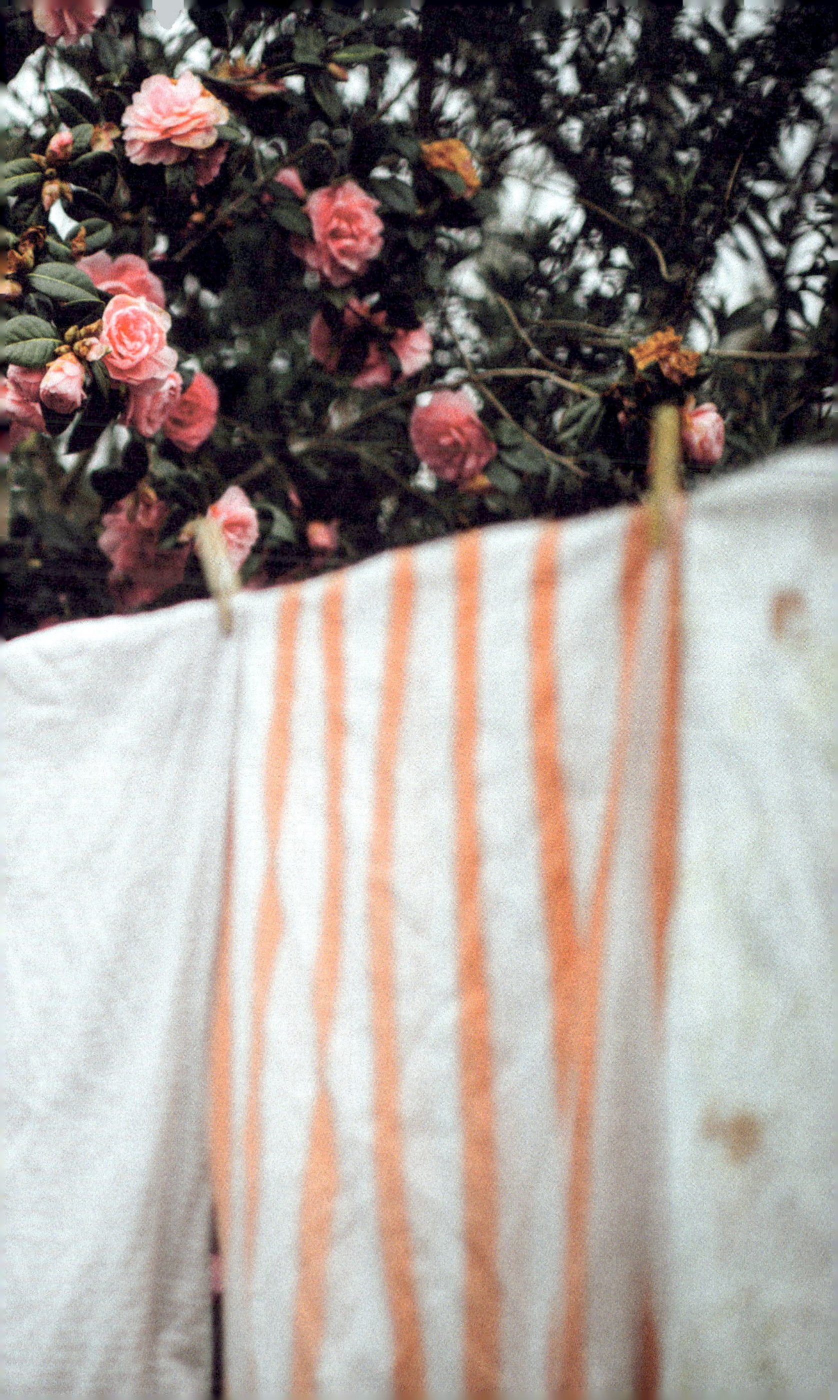

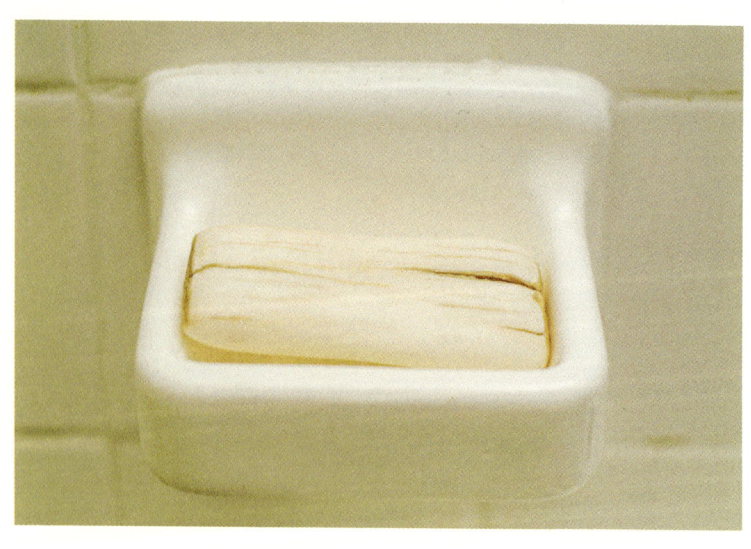

Previous: Polly Alderton, 2020
Above: Anthony Masterson, 2007

THE PATIENCE OF ORDINARY THINGS

It is a kind of love, is it not?
How the cup holds the tea,
How the chair stands sturdy and foursquare,
How the floor receives the bottoms of shoes
Or toes. How soles of feet know
Where they're supposed to be.
I've been thinking about the patience
Of ordinary things, how clothes
Wait respectfully in closets
And soap dries quietly in the dish,
And towels drink the wet
From the skin of the back.
And the lovely repetition of stairs.
And what is more generous than a window?

— *Pat Schneider*

Right: Julia Forsman, 2016

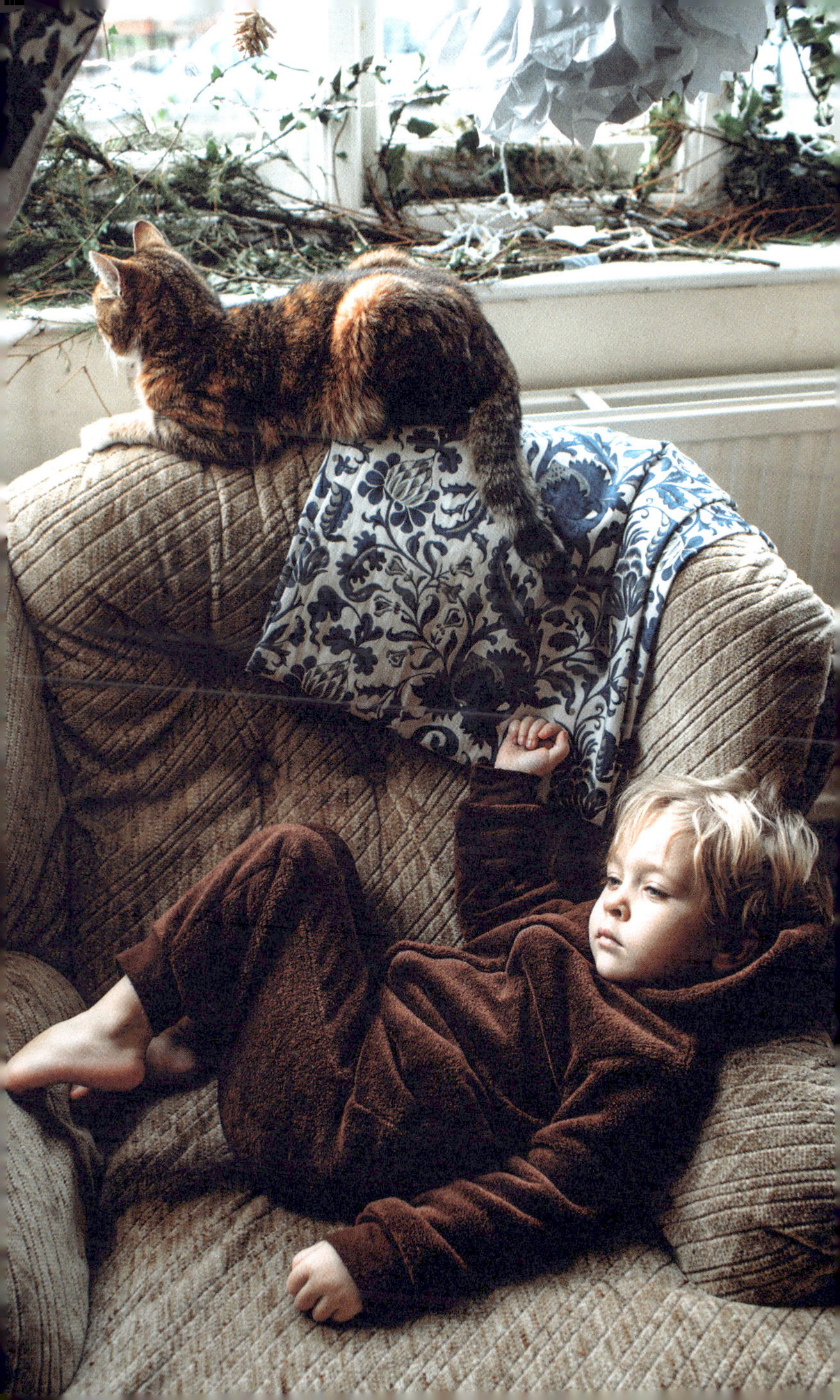

Practice 1

SENSORY CHECK-IN

In moments when we feel overwhelmed by all the demands a household can place on our attention, a quick inventory of our five senses can be a calming exercise. It's also a way of perking up the different antennae we have for experiencing wonder all around us.

What can you see?

e.g. a book, a plant, a cat

What can you touch?

e.g. a woollen sweater, a cork table mat, a steel sink

What you can hear?

e.g. traffic outside, the fridge humming, rain on the window

What can you smell?

e.g. a cup of coffee, a bar of soap, a candle

What can you taste?

e.g. a glass of water, a slice of lemon, a bowl of soup

Practice 2

DO BE DO BE DO

To do is to be. — Socrates
To be is to do. — Jean-Paul Sartre
Do be do be do. — Frank Sinatra
— public toilet graffiti

It can be difficult to find stillness at home. Rather than set yourself lofty meditation goals, have a go at this do-be-do-be-do exercise.

The instructions are simple: pause in the middle of whatever you are doing and be still for a moment. You might be halfway up the stairs or midway through making a sandwich. It only needs to be a brief pause, enough to remind yourself that you are a human *being* as well as a human *doing*.

If it helps, set a regular reminder to pause on your phone (a gentle chime or bell rather than an unpleasantly loud buzzer). Monastics across many traditions have used bells to call for a sacred pause. You are not trying to turn your home into a monastery – only to remember it's not a factory.

If you think you don't have time to pause, take note of this Zen proverb: 'You should sit in meditation for 20 minutes every day – unless you're too busy; then you should sit for an hour.'

Practice 3

LIGHTSTALKING

Awareness of light is almost like a sixth sense.
— Laura Pashby, *Little Stories of Your Life*

Watch the sunlight as it moves into, through and out of your home over the course of the day. Notice how it first enters, slipping through blinds or flooding around the edges of curtains. Observe the patterns and shadows it makes on walls and floors and how these change from morning to afternoon to evening.

If you want, you can write about it, take photographs or even a video that documents how light changes everything it touches. Or you could just bask in the warmth of the light or the cool of the shadows, doing nothing except noticing and appreciating this most fundamental wonder on which all other life depends.

Practice 4

THE SECRET LIFE OF THINGS

Look around at the inanimate objects in one room of your home. Try to write down *everything* that you see. In the bathroom, this might include a light switch, two towels, a bath mat, cork tiles, the basin and bath, the taps, the shower head, three shampoo bottles, two toothbrushes and so on. Include all of it without any hierarchy.

Pick random objects from the list and try to imagine what they have seen, heard or felt. What did the mirror see when you looked into it this morning? What did the slippers hear while they were waiting in the corner of the room? What did the drain feel as it swallowed down the bathwater? What about the towel left in a heap on the floor? Or the window as it lets the light in?

Are you sure that objects don't have feelings? Children often attribute animate thoughts to inanimate objects. As grown-ups, we tend to dismiss this as silly, but it's fun to release ourselves from received ideas about what makes sense and what doesn't. Artists often use exercises like this one to limber up their imaginations. Have a go and see if some of the things in your home start to take on a new life.

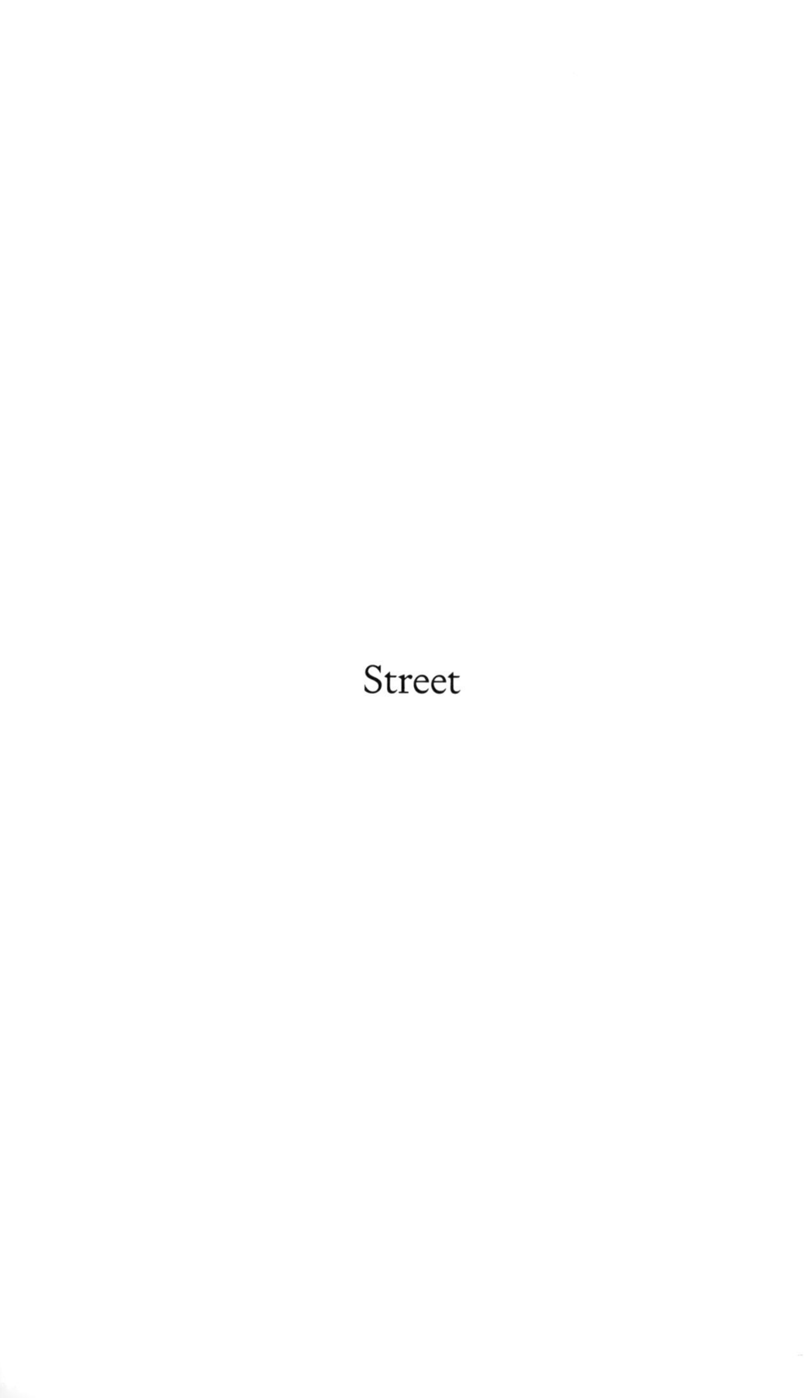

Street

When we step out of our front door, we exchange the privacy of home for the communality of the street: a jumble of people and patterns, energy and encounters. Here, the two-footed, the four-footed, the winged and the wheeled weave around one another in an ever-changing smorgasbord of wonder.

The photographs and poems in this chapter reveal the street in glimpses and snatches: a flash of lights, a puff of smoke, a whiff of food, a furtive glance. We read of a father carefully carrying his sleeping son across the road and strangers blessing one another when they sneeze. We see patterns made by peeling paint and plastic hoardings and imagine a strange orchestra created by traffic, birdsong, construction and conversation.

Sometimes life on the street feels messy or banal, but on other days, we might sense a kind of holiness in this miscellany of cracks and cables, wires and weeds, puddles and railings, sirens and strangers. There are days when we must keep our heads down, getting from A to B. But occasionally, we can let ourselves drift a little, delighting in the choreography of lines, shapes, colours, shadows and reflections, moved by the tension and tenderness between so many different humans going about their business.

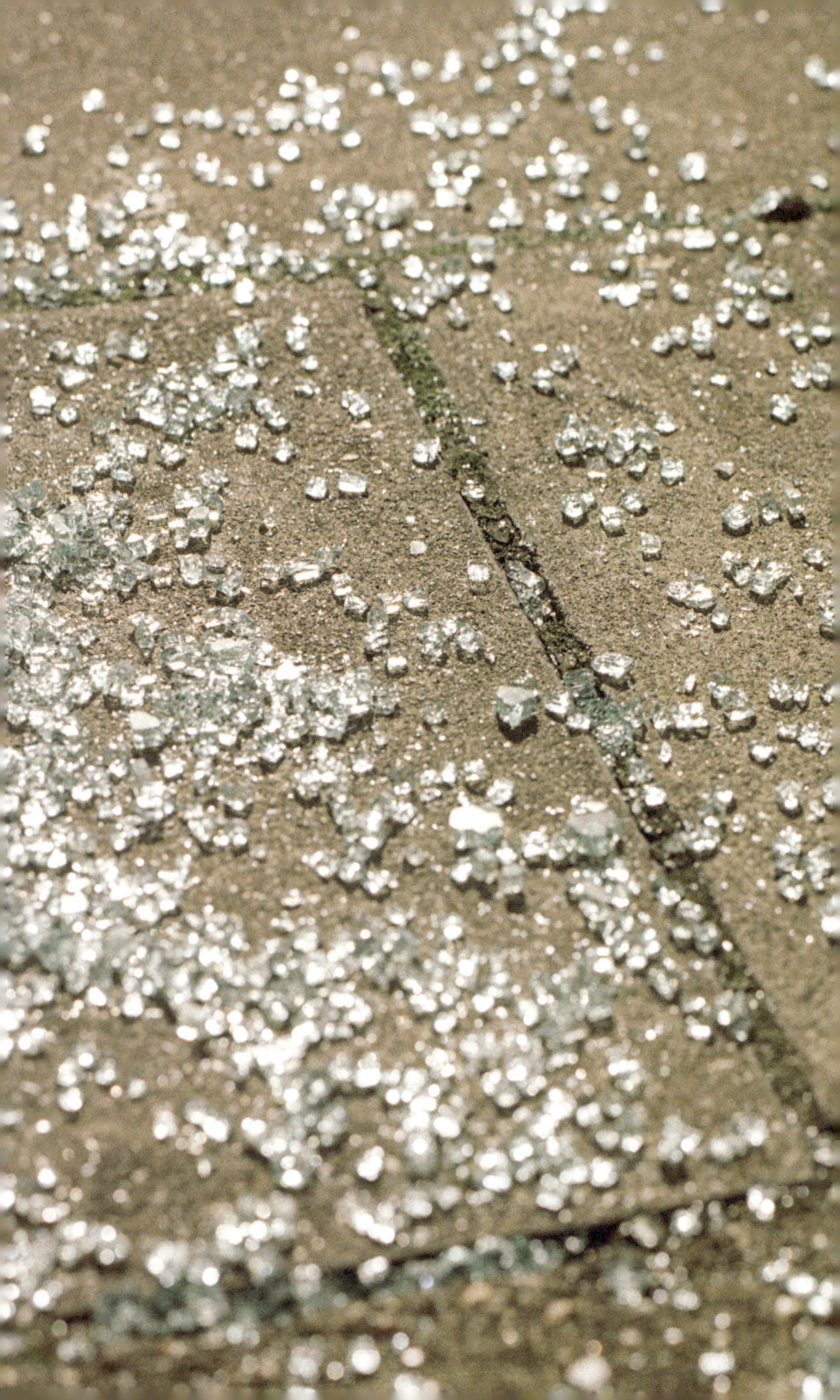

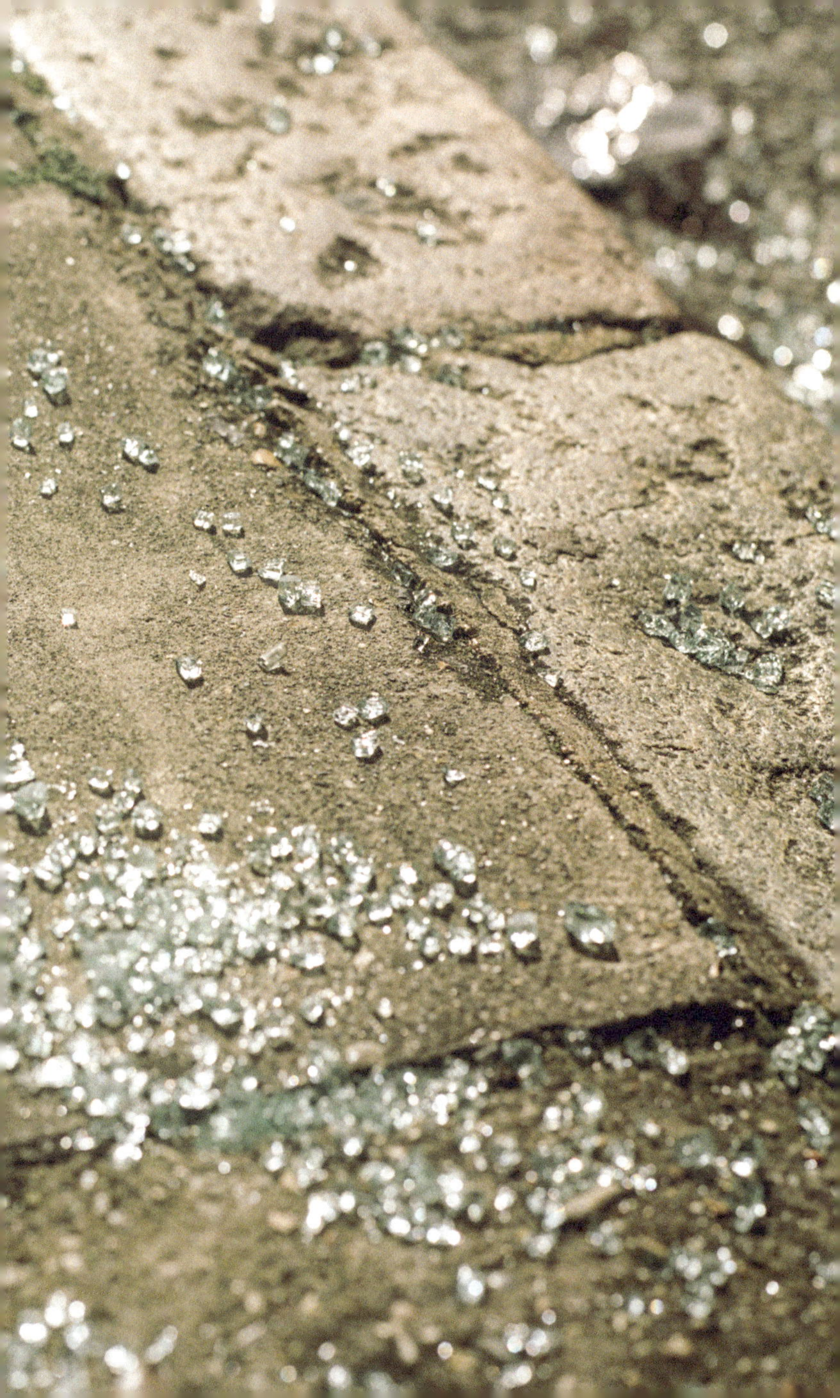

Previous: Freya Najade, *Broken Glass*, 2023
Overleaf: Melissa O'Shaughnessy, *Rivington Street, New York*, 2019

SMALL KINDNESSES

I've been thinking about the way, when you walk
down a crowded aisle, people pull in their legs
to let you by. Or how strangers still say "bless you"
when someone sneezes, a leftover
from the Bubonic plague. "Don't die," we are saying.
And sometimes, when you spill lemons
from your grocery bag, someone else will help you
pick them up. Mostly, we don't want to harm each other.
We want to be handed our cup of coffee hot,
and to say thank you to the person handing it. To smile
at them and for them to smile back. For the waitress
to call us honey when she sets down the bowl of clam chowder,
and for the driver in the red pick-up truck to let us pass.
We have so little of each other, now. So far
from tribe and fire. Only these brief moments of exchange.
What if they are the true dwelling of the holy, these
fleeting temples we make together when we say, "Here,
have my seat," "Go ahead—you first," "I like your hat."

— *Danusha Laméris*

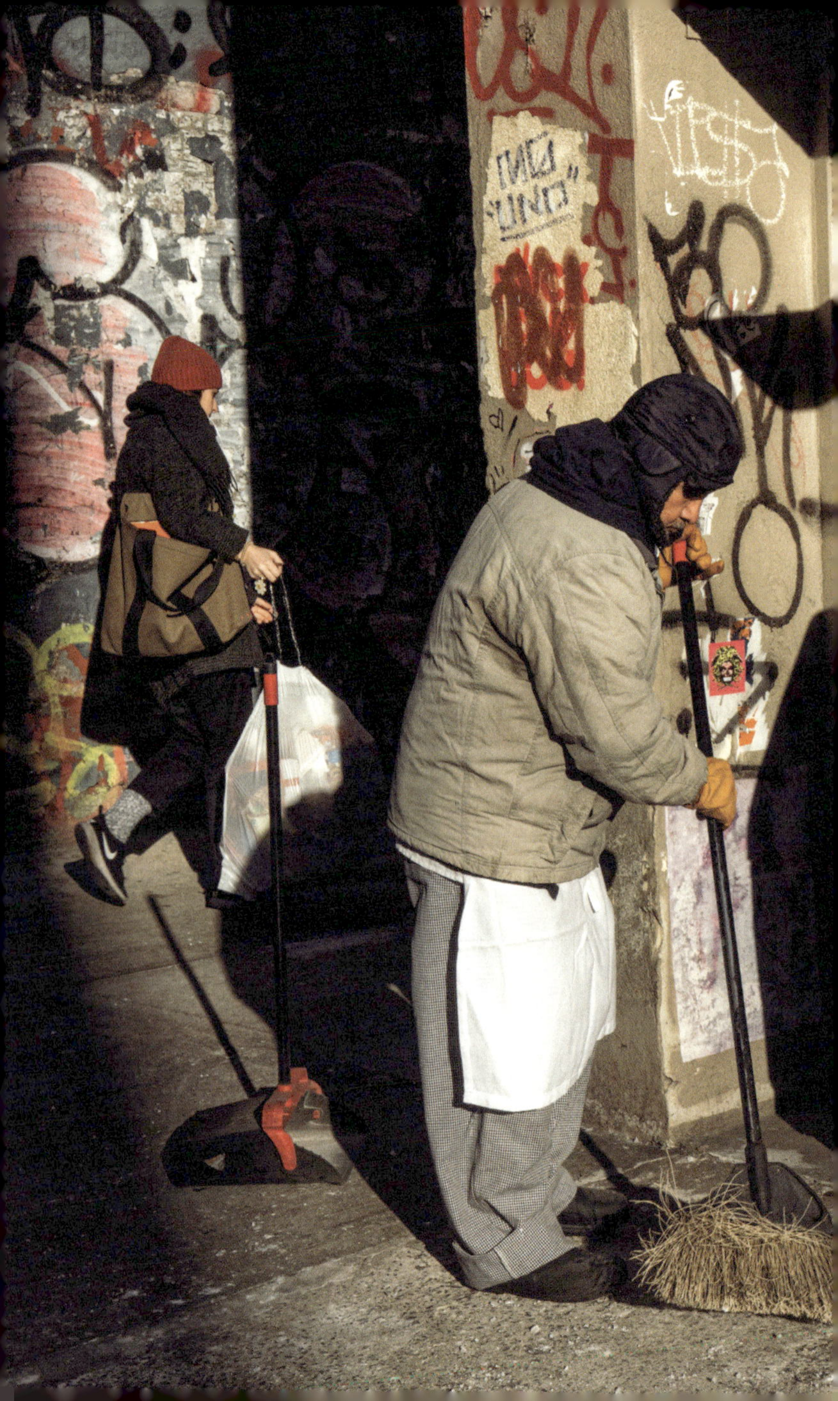

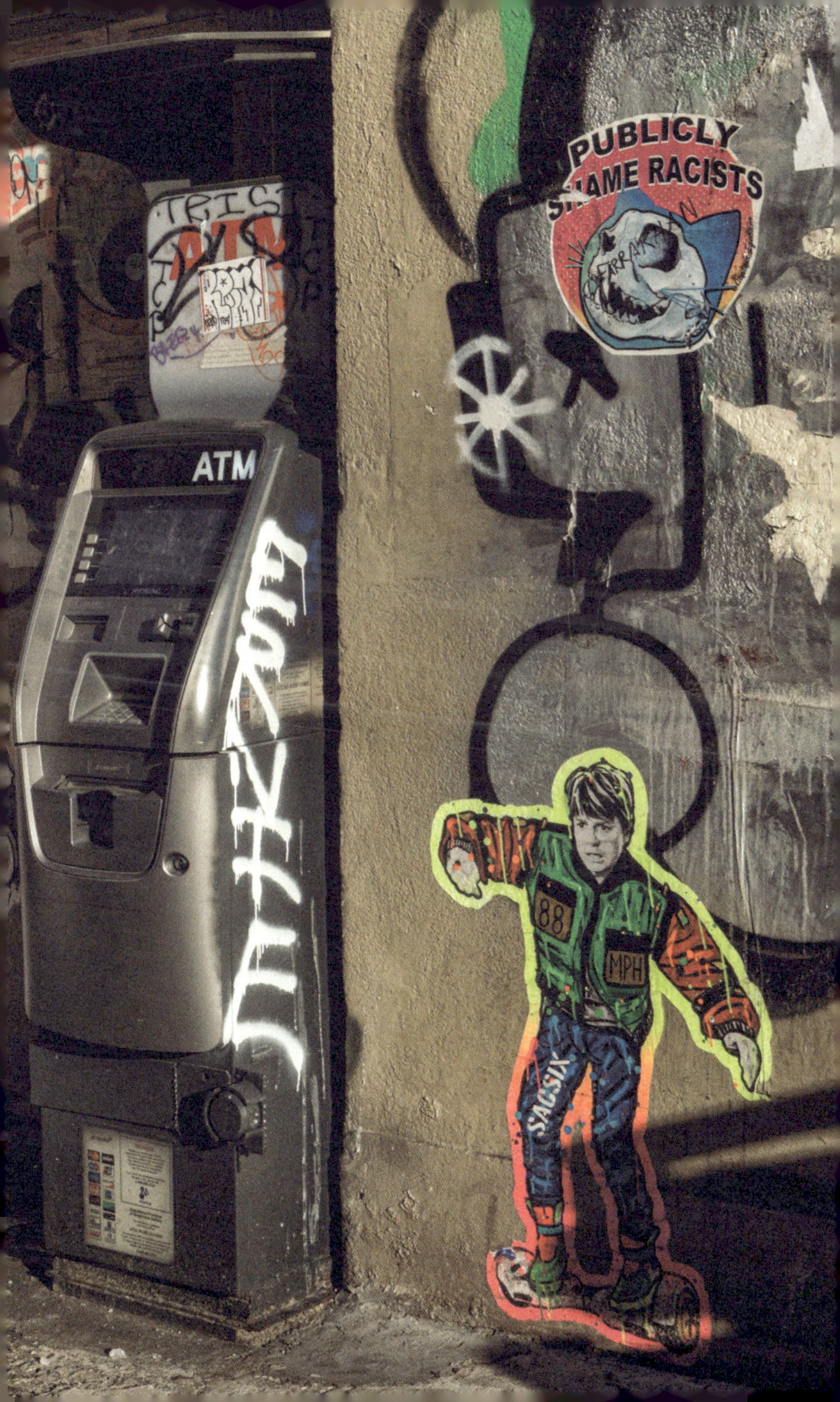
PUBLICLY
SHAME RACISTS
ATM
88
MPH
SAGSIX

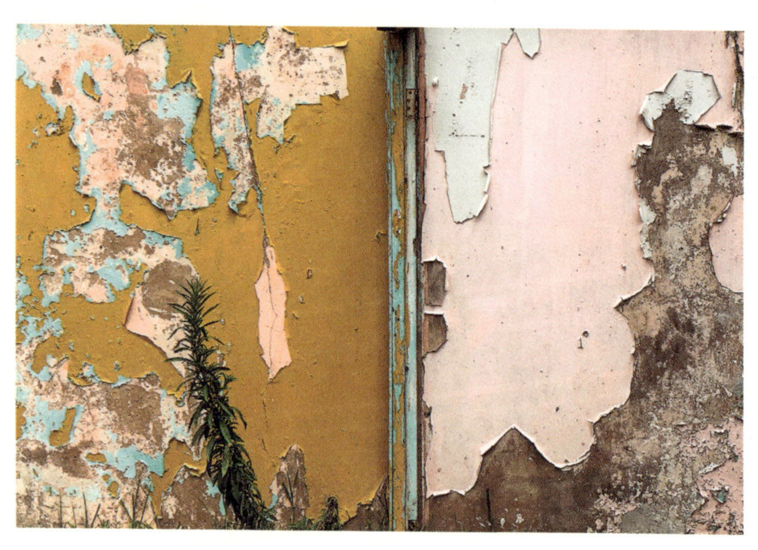

Gil Walker, *Switch to Pink*, 2022

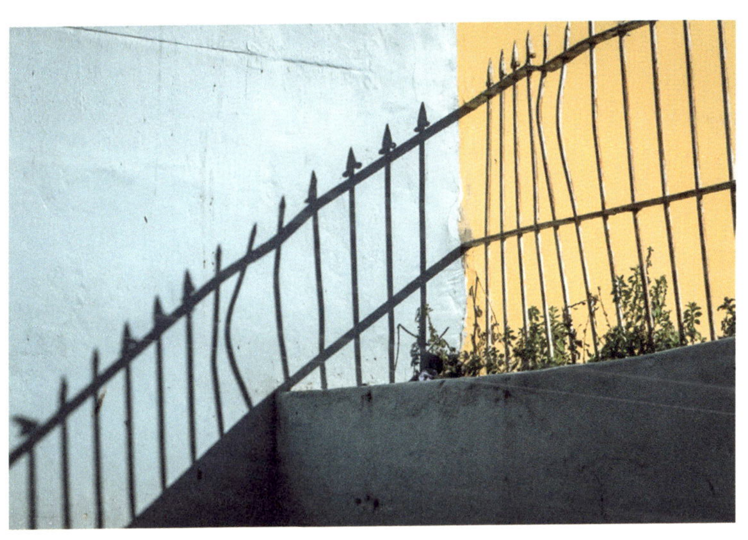

Gil Walker, *Lightbender*, 2019

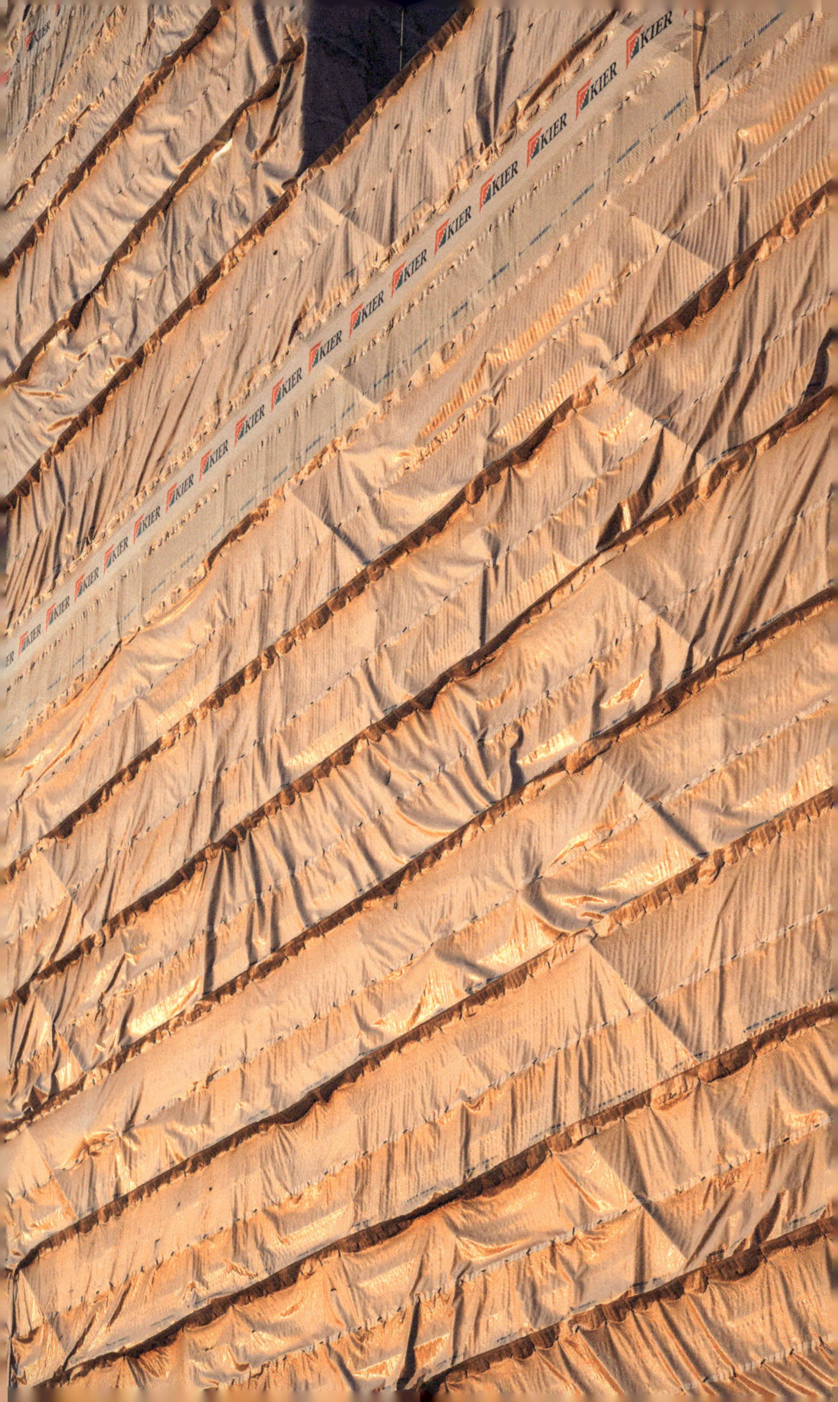
KIER

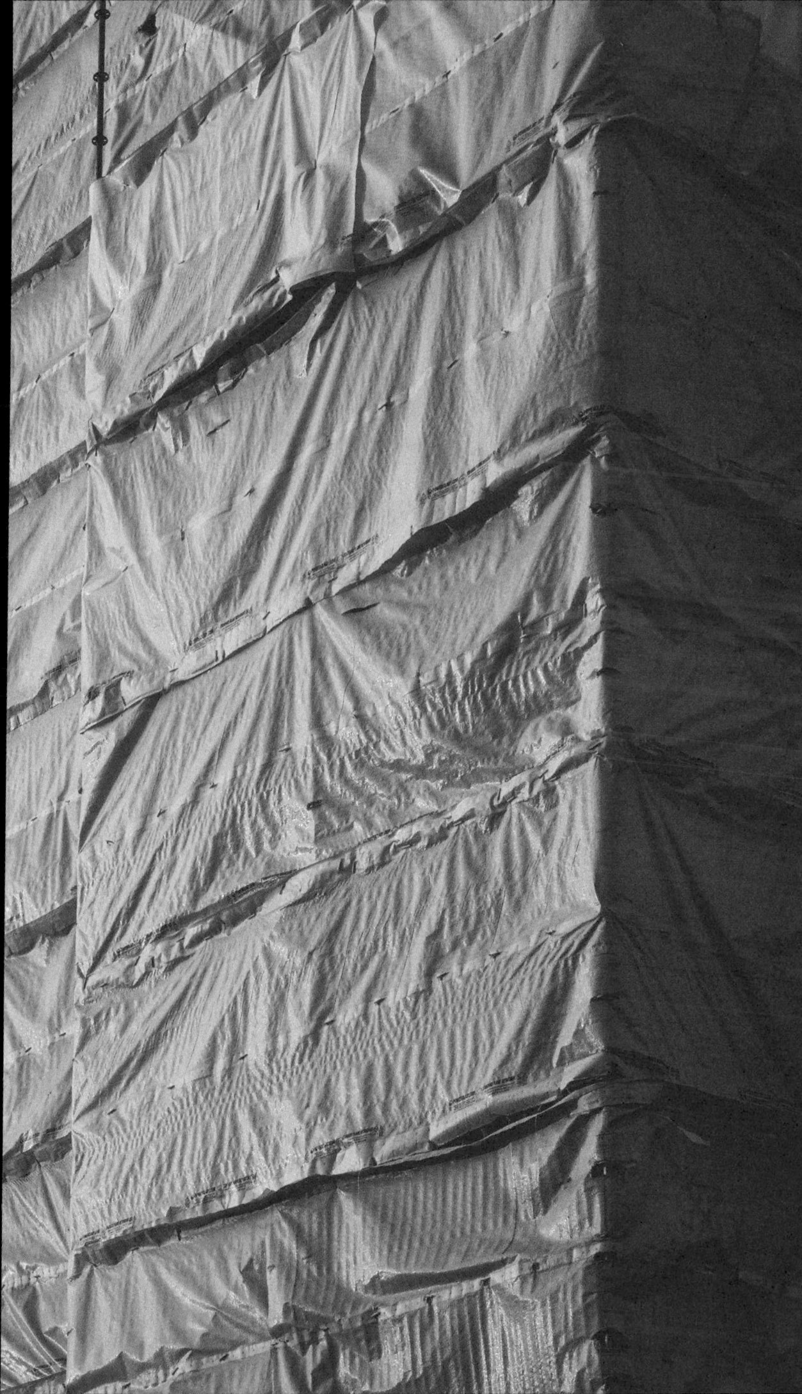

Previous: Greg White, 2021

SHOULDERS

A man crosses the street in rain,
stepping gently, looking two times north and south,
because his son is asleep on his shoulder.

No car must splash him.
No car drive too near to his shadow.

This man carries the world's most sensitive cargo
but he's not marked.
Nowhere does his jacket say FRAGILE,
HANDLE WITH CARE.

His ear fills up with breathing.
He hears the hum of a boy's dream
deep inside him.

We're not going to be able
to live in this world
if we're not willing to do what he's doing
with one another.

The road will only be wide.
The rain will never stop falling.

— *Naomi Shihab Nye*

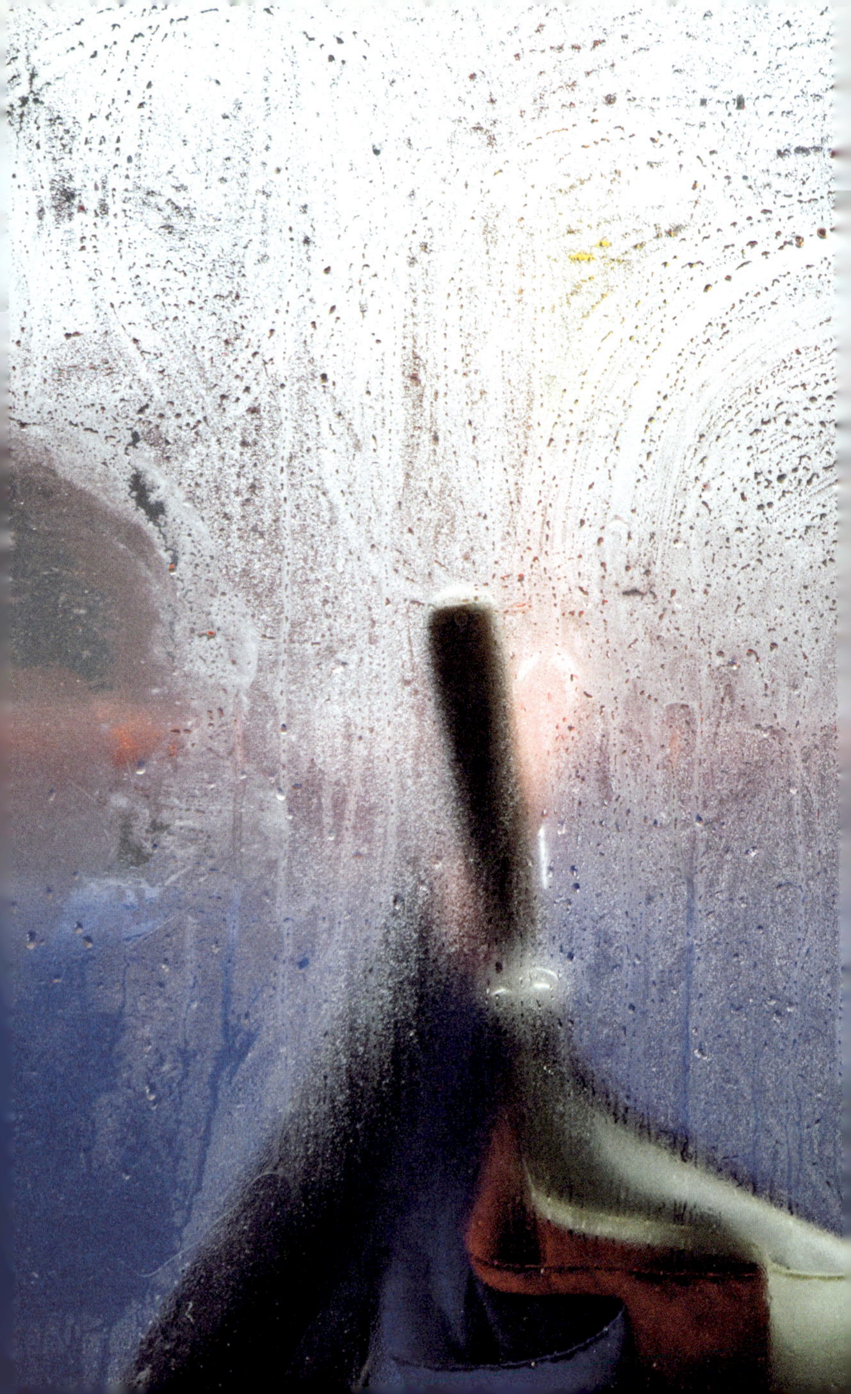

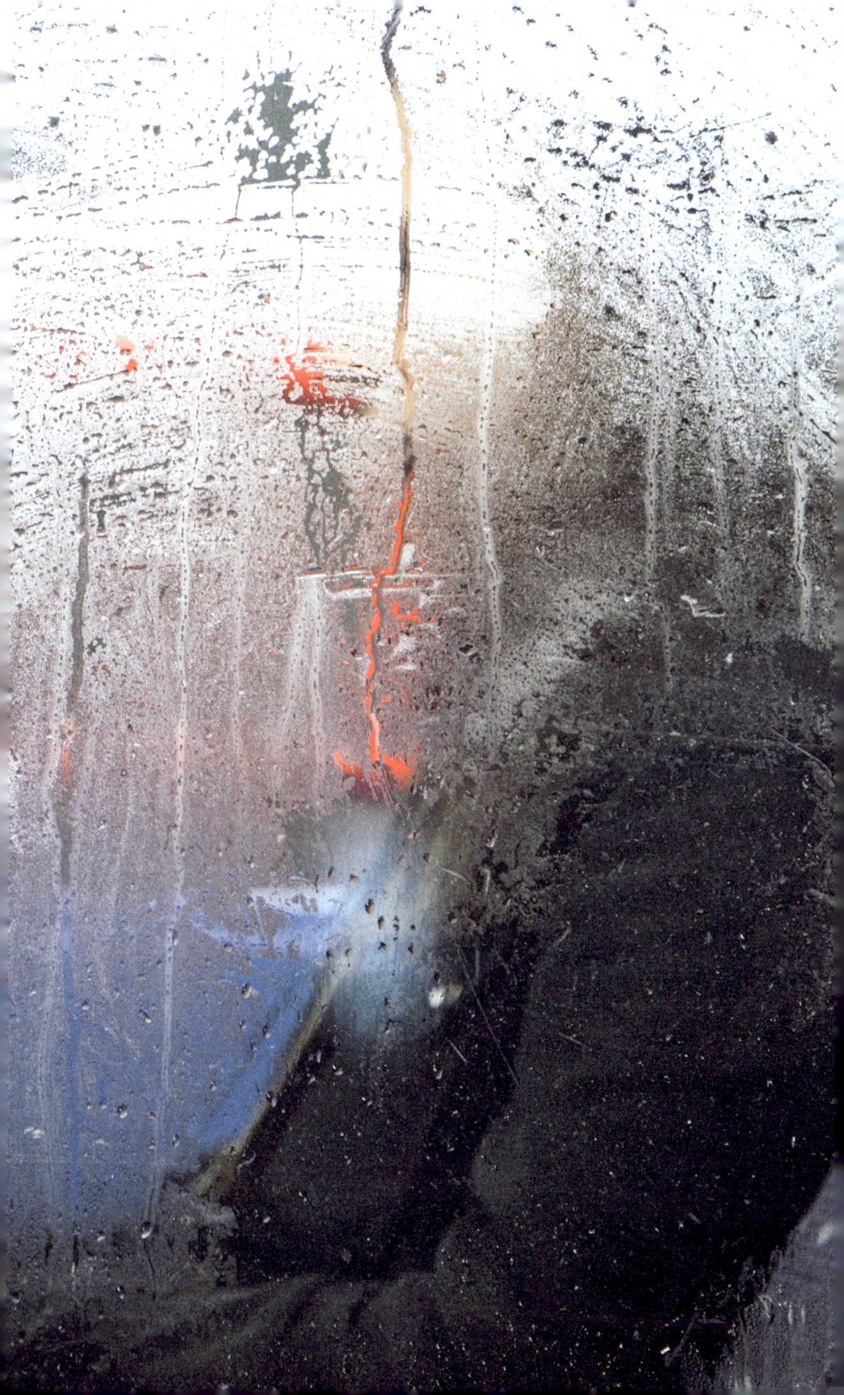

Previous: Nick Turpin, *Through A Glass Darkly* #12, 2017

THE BLUE UMBRELLA

Today I saw a woman
Fold up her blue umbrella
And step out into the rain.
She lifted her lovely face.
Soft,
So softly,
She closed her eyes and smiled.
Drops of water slipped down,
Running over and around
Her warm, grateful lids,
Sliding down her cheeks
Like unchecked tears.
After a moment or two
She walked on
(Without putting up her umbrella).
Leaving me beached and breathless,
Feeling as if I had just witnessed
Perhaps the finest prayer
Ever prayed.

— *Carrie Newcomer*

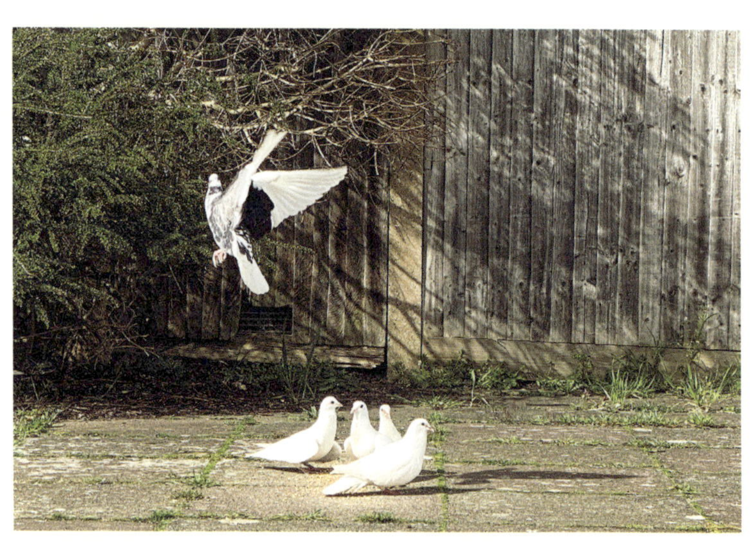

Kathryn Martin, *Serendipity*, 2022

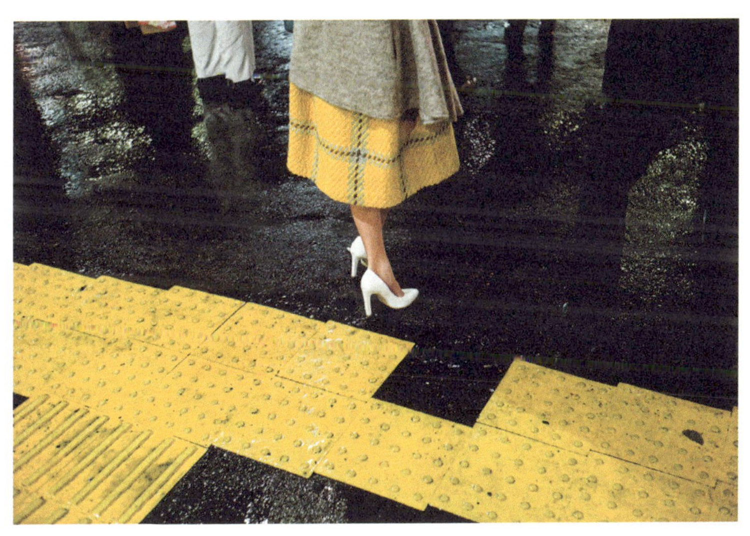

Shin Noguchi, *Shinjuku, Tokyo*, 2016

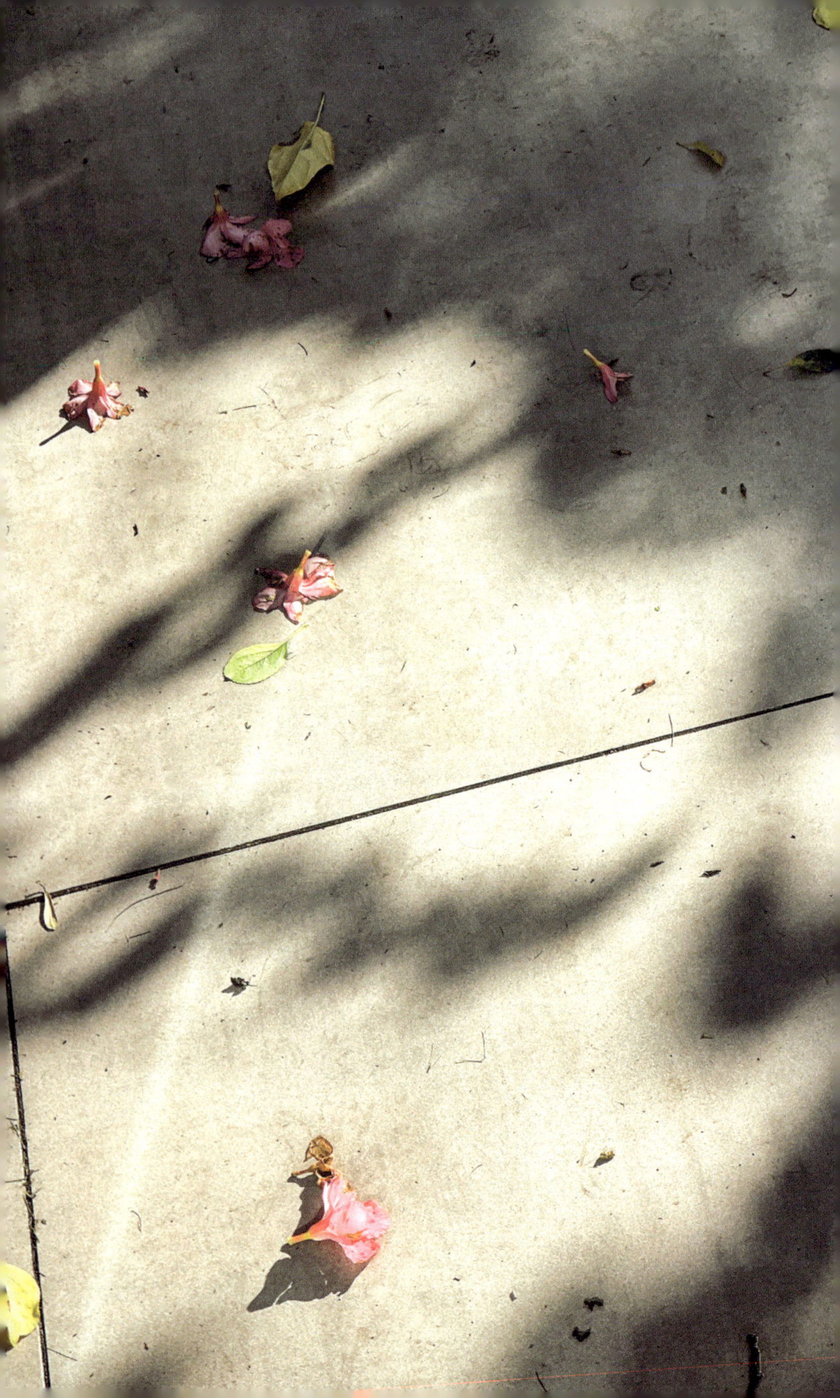

PRAYING

It doesn't have to be
the blue iris, it could be
weeds in a vacant lot, or a few
small stones; just
pay attention, then patch

a few words together and don't try
to make them elaborate, this isn't
a contest but the doorway

into thanks, and a silence in which
another voice may speak.

— *Mary Oliver*

Left: Jenny Lewis, *Remnant*, 2023

Practice 1

AN AWE WALK

Awe is the feeling we get in the presence of something vast and unknowable. It's often associated with dramatic natural wonders, but you don't need to head to the Alps or the Grand Canyon to experience its strange tingle. In a curious state of mind, you can feel plenty of awe walking down an ordinary street.

Try to set out free from as many obligations and distractions as possible – no friends, no dogs, no errands, no phone. The aim is to let your mind become a blank slate, receptive to whatever you encounter. Allow yourself to be drawn in by whatever attracts, confuses or delights you – the reflections in a puddle, the shadows cast by railings, the unpredictable jumble of civic codes, signs and symbols. Go as slowly as you dare, like a toddler fascinated by everything. You needn't travel far, but if you get a bit lost, so much the better. Awe bristles at the edge of what's known.

Try this exercise at night, too, when artificial lighting and nocturnal creatures can make familiar streets feel suddenly mysterious.

Practice 2

UNKNOWN LIVES

The people. The people. Everyone looks so exalted, or so wretched, or so spiffy, so funny, so splendid. If you are ever bored or blue, stand on the street corner for half an hour.
— Maira Kalman, *The Principles of Uncertainty*

You can do this exercise pretty much anywhere: in a cafe, on a park bench, inside a train station or even, as artist Maira Kalman suggests, on a street corner. Just commit to spending half an hour watching people passing by. Notice the emotions on their faces – the glimpses of hope, sadness, anxiety, joy or boredom. Observe the body language between friends, families, lovers and strangers – hands held and released, collisions avoided or apologised for, bodies awkward or intimate together. Imagine where people might be going, what could be on their minds, what might be in their bags, even what their names could be. Every stranger has a story full of complexity and challenge. It's humbling to be reminded how little we know of another.

Practice 3

SMALL KINDNESSES

Inspired by Danusha Laméris's poem on p.47, wander the streets looking for signs of civility and care. Notice the small interactions between people: the way someone holds open a door, lets a stranger go in front of them, helps carry a pram up some stairs or just says 'thank you'. Look for the interventions people have made to ease or enliven each other's journey through public space – a helpful ramp, a friendly sign or a witty piece of graffiti.

It's easy to buy into a story that we are all in too much of a rush to look out for one another. In fact, we are mostly polite and often considerate, and in adversity, we tend to look out for one another. Laméris reminds us that kindness doesn't have to be something grand or extravagant. The smallest gestures of care or compassion can transform our sense of belonging.

Practice 4

LOST AND FOUND

Wrappers and white goods, fag-ends and furniture, gloves, cans, umbrellas and bills: there's a strange serendipity to all the stuff that gets abandoned on the street. Some of it is litter; other things are accidentally dropped; larger items are often intentionally fly-tipped. It can feel like a rather sad commentary on our throwaway consumer culture. But there are also signs of wonder here: in the 'please take' signs and spontaneous lending libraries, in giveaways that prevent things from going to waste or in the care people take to hang up lost keys for others to retrieve.

We don't know the stories behind most discarded objects, but we can have fun speculating. Next time you come across a lonely glove or a stray pair of glasses, pause and consider what its story might be. A sandwich may have been chucked in disgust after a single bite or dropped mistakenly, much to someone's dismay. A scarf may have been loved for years before it slipped off or dumped in a fury after a sports defeat. It's up to us whether to look at these things with a detective's lens, a comedian's wit or a poet's eye.

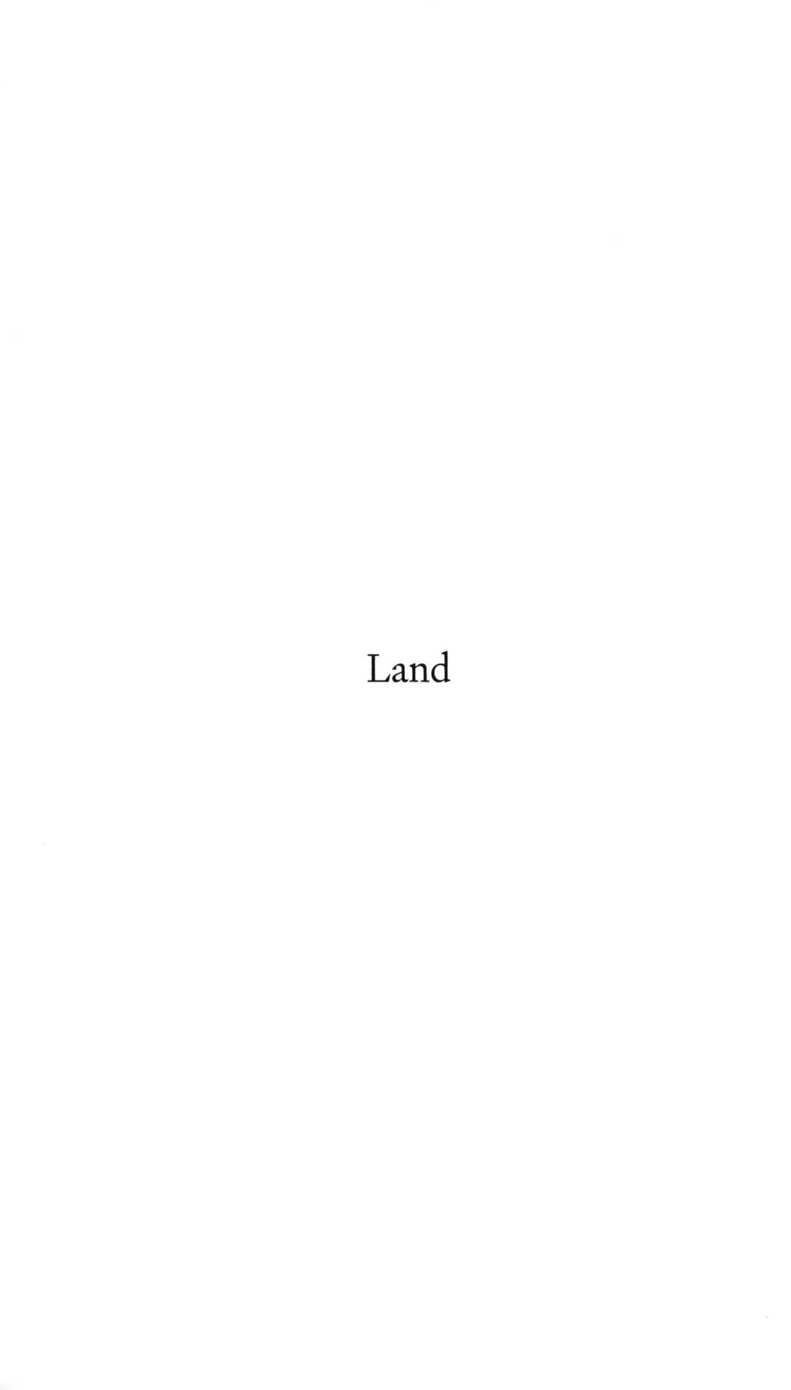

Land

It can feel clichéd to view the land as a source of wonder. After all, this is where we encounter snow, starlings and sunsets. But it's also where we find mud, slugs and snails. Here are poems and photographs that invite us not only to marvel at big skies and changing seasons but also to sink our hands into the soil, brush our legs against the dew and let insects crawl over our skin.

The word humility comes from the Latin *humus*, meaning earth. Often, it's when we're closest to the ground that we feel most humbled by it. We needn't understand everything going on as we're trampling through brambles or listening to birds; an attitude of wonder is often an acknowledgement of how little we know. When we hold a newly harvested potato, watch a snail hauling itself onto a mushroom or gaze through the branching patterns of winter trees, we may sense that we are glimpsing complex and awe-inspiring ecologies.

We don't have to travel far to witness the ordinary miracles of nature; they are there in our back gardens, urban parks and roadside hedgerows. As we get intimate with the wildlife all around us, it's good to remember that we ourselves are part of this breathing, digesting, blossoming, composting and multiplying web of life.

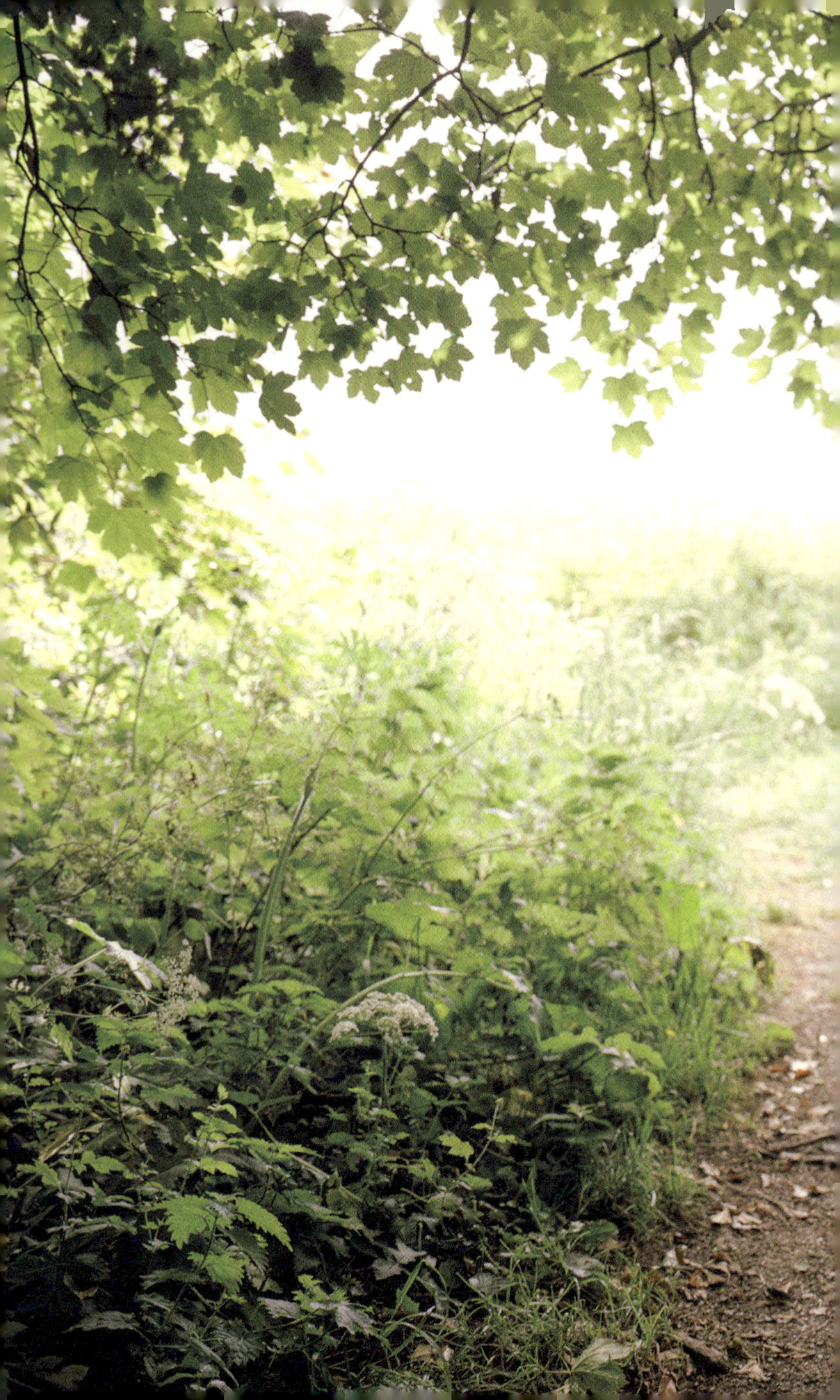

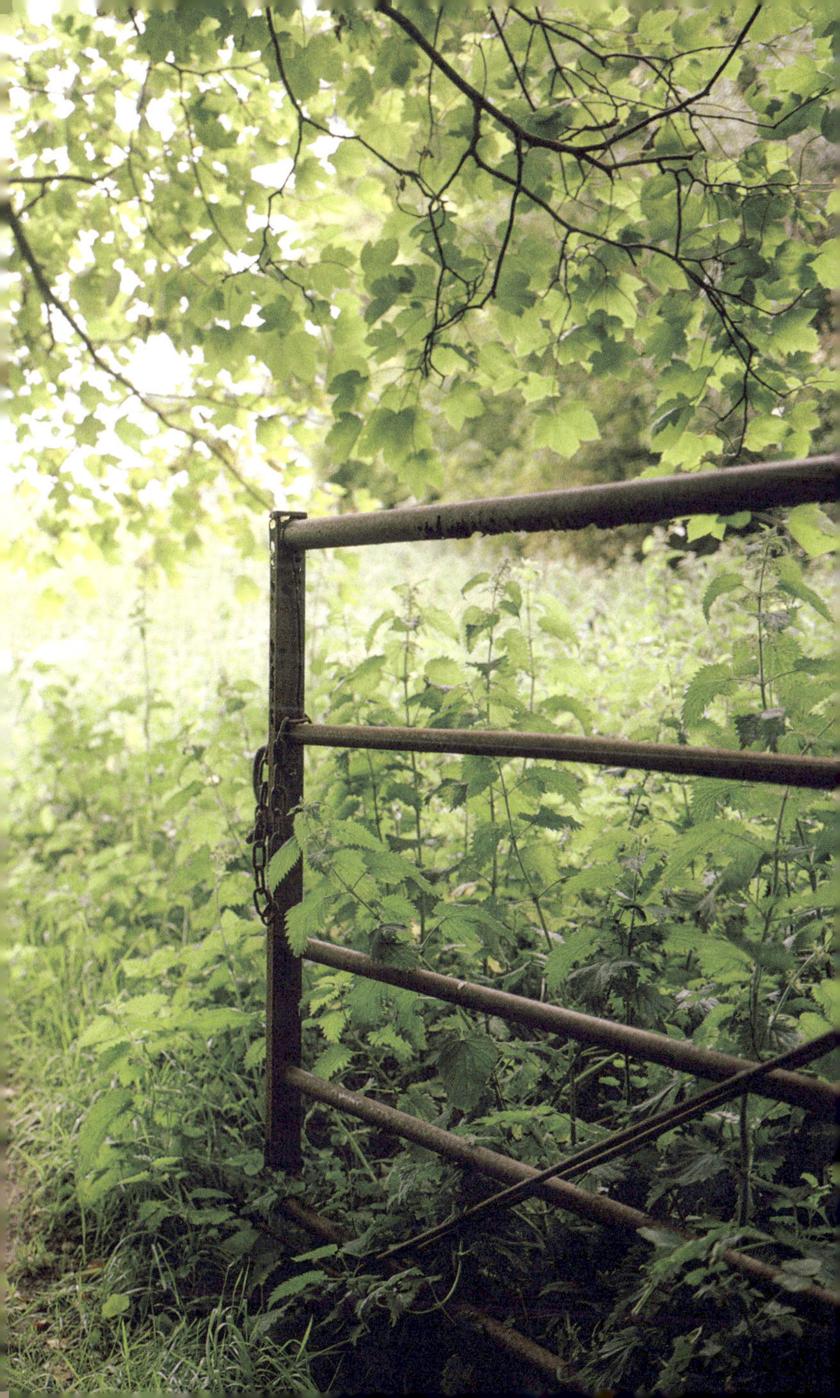

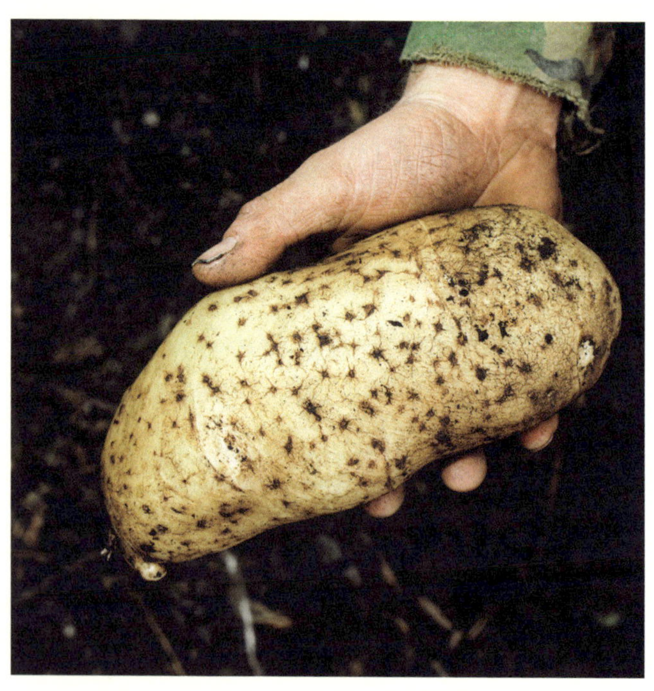

Previous: Niall McDiarmid, *Maiden Bradley, Wiltshire*, 2020
Above: Tessa Bunney, *Howardian Hills, North Yorkshire, England*, 2016

THE GODDESS OF NOTHING AT ALL

The goddess of nothing at all
came to offer me succulent
morsels of ordinary life
tasting like honey.
It was a most curious thing.
I, with my colossal ambition
and a misunderstanding about
what's tin or gold
dismissed them as
just another day.

— *Josie George*

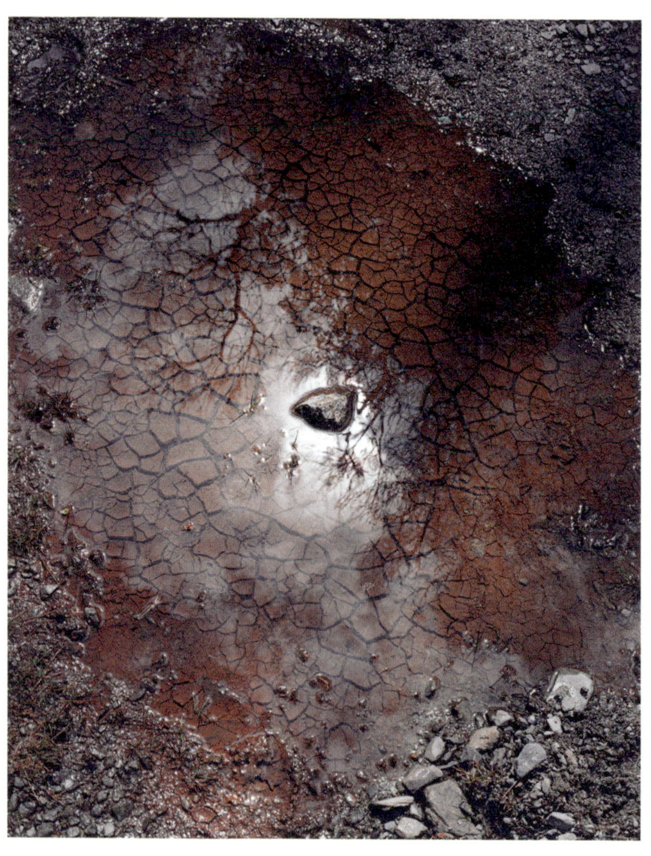

Robin Friend, *Hodge Close Quarry, Coniston, England*, 2010

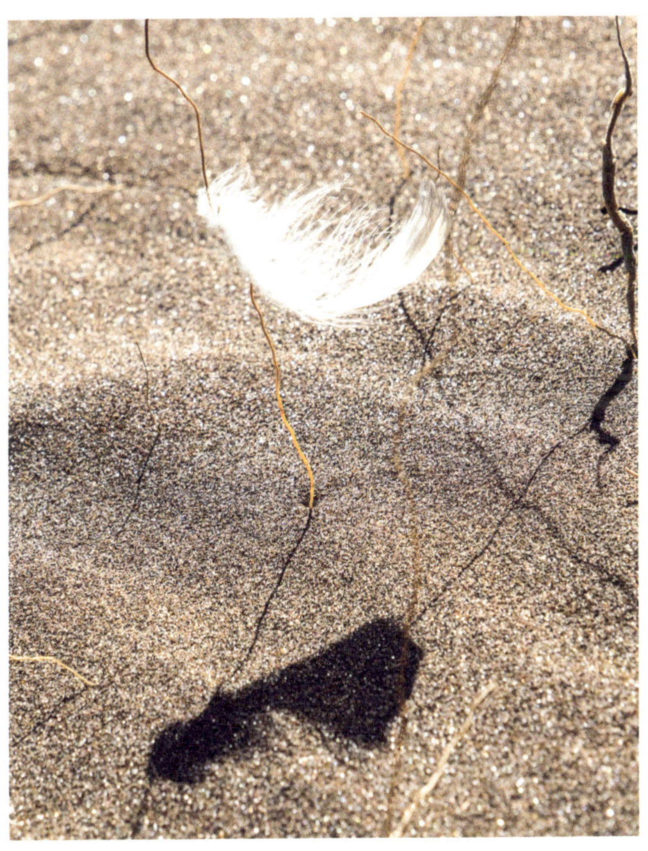

Colleen Williams, *Tiny Feather*, 2024

REINCARNATE

I want to come back as that ordinary
garden snail, carting my brown-striped spiral shell
onto the mushroom which has sprouted
after overnight rain so I can stretch
my tentacles toward the slightly drooping
and pimpled raspberry, sweet and pulsing —
a thumb that bends on its stalk from the crown
of small leaves, weighed down by the almost
translucent shining drop of dew I have
been reaching and reaching toward my whole life.

— *Patricia Fargnoli*

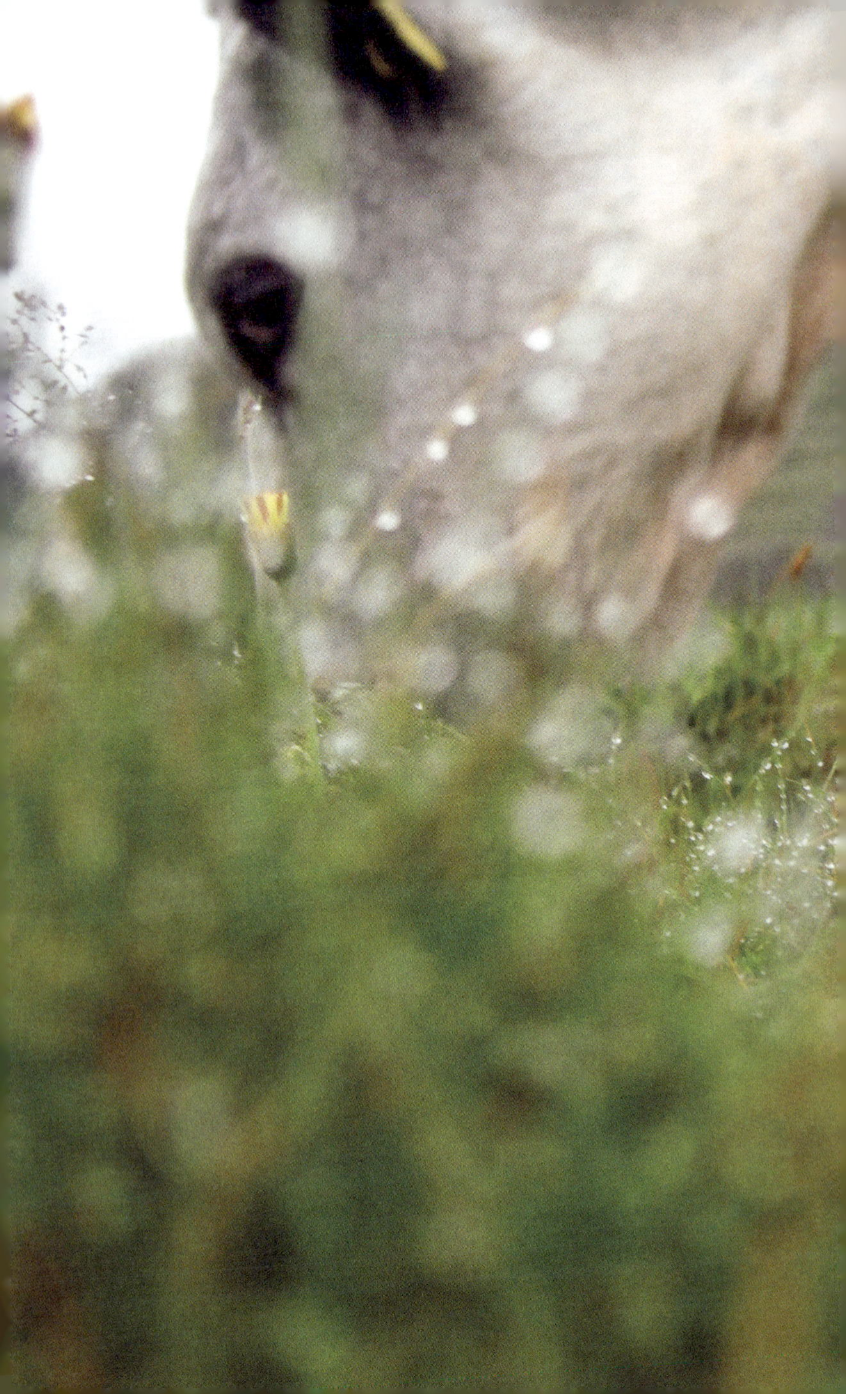

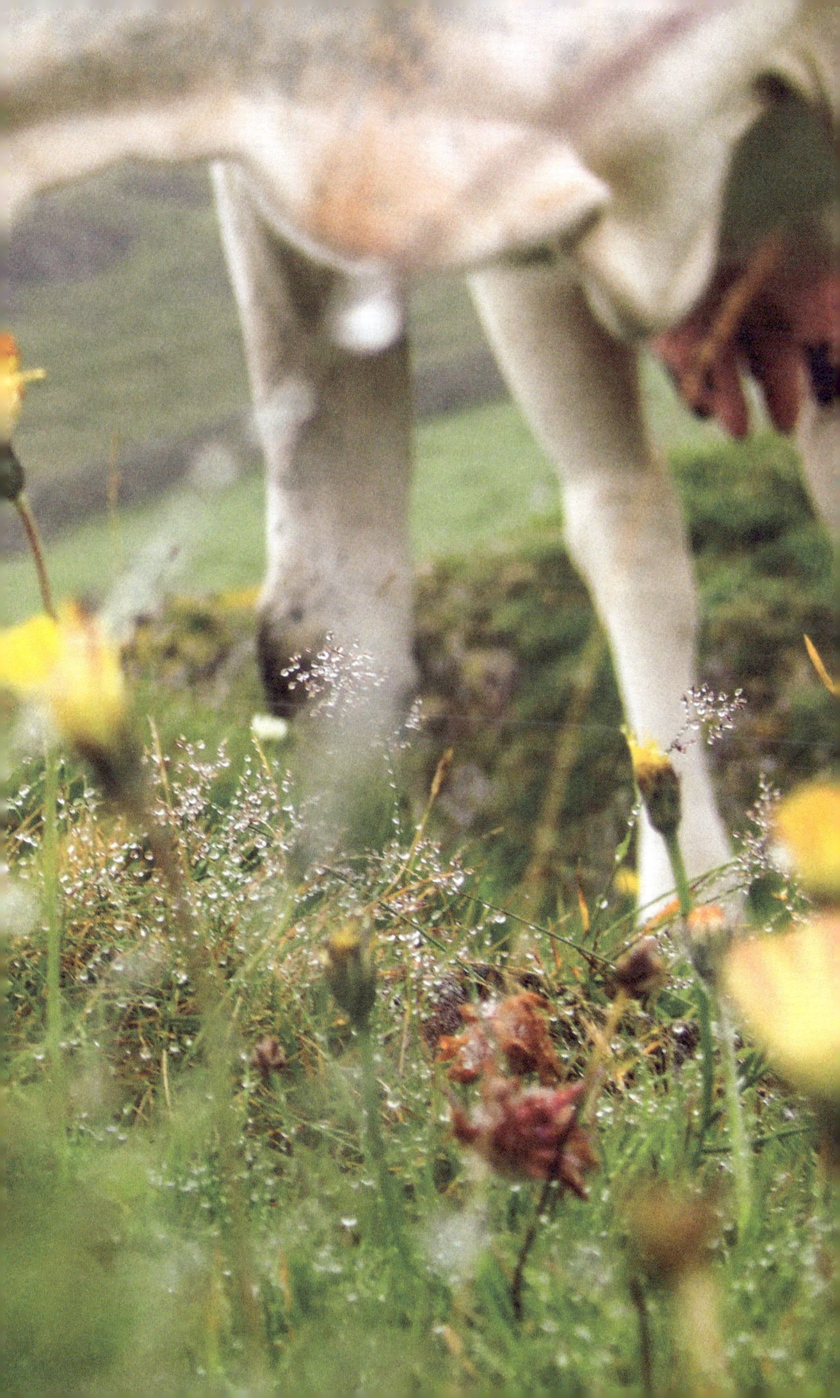

Previous: Kate Kirkwood, *Cow in Morning Dew*, 2017
Above: Freya Najade, *Sky over Hackney*, 2023

STICK SEASON

Just when I think nothing can help,
the flash of a bluebird in brambles
comforts me, that velvety piece of sky
with every sweep of its wing feathers
softening the sharp hours of this time
we call stick season here. Even the fallen
maple consoles, with its patches of moss
and stepladder of fungi climbing out of
what was once so towering and alive.
Even holes made by woodpeckers, which
weakened the trunk, even the crumbling
heartwood already returning to earth.

— *James Crews*

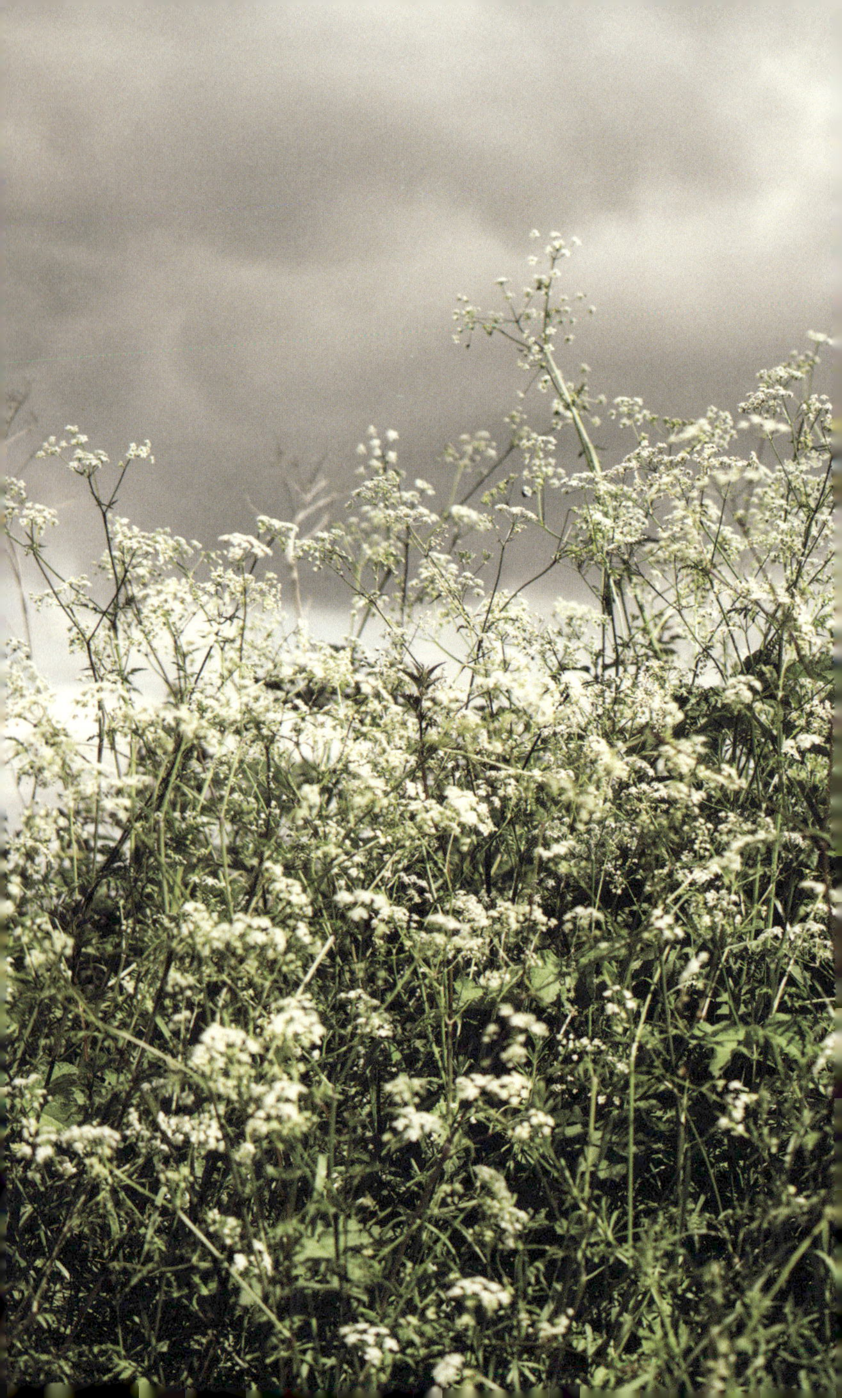

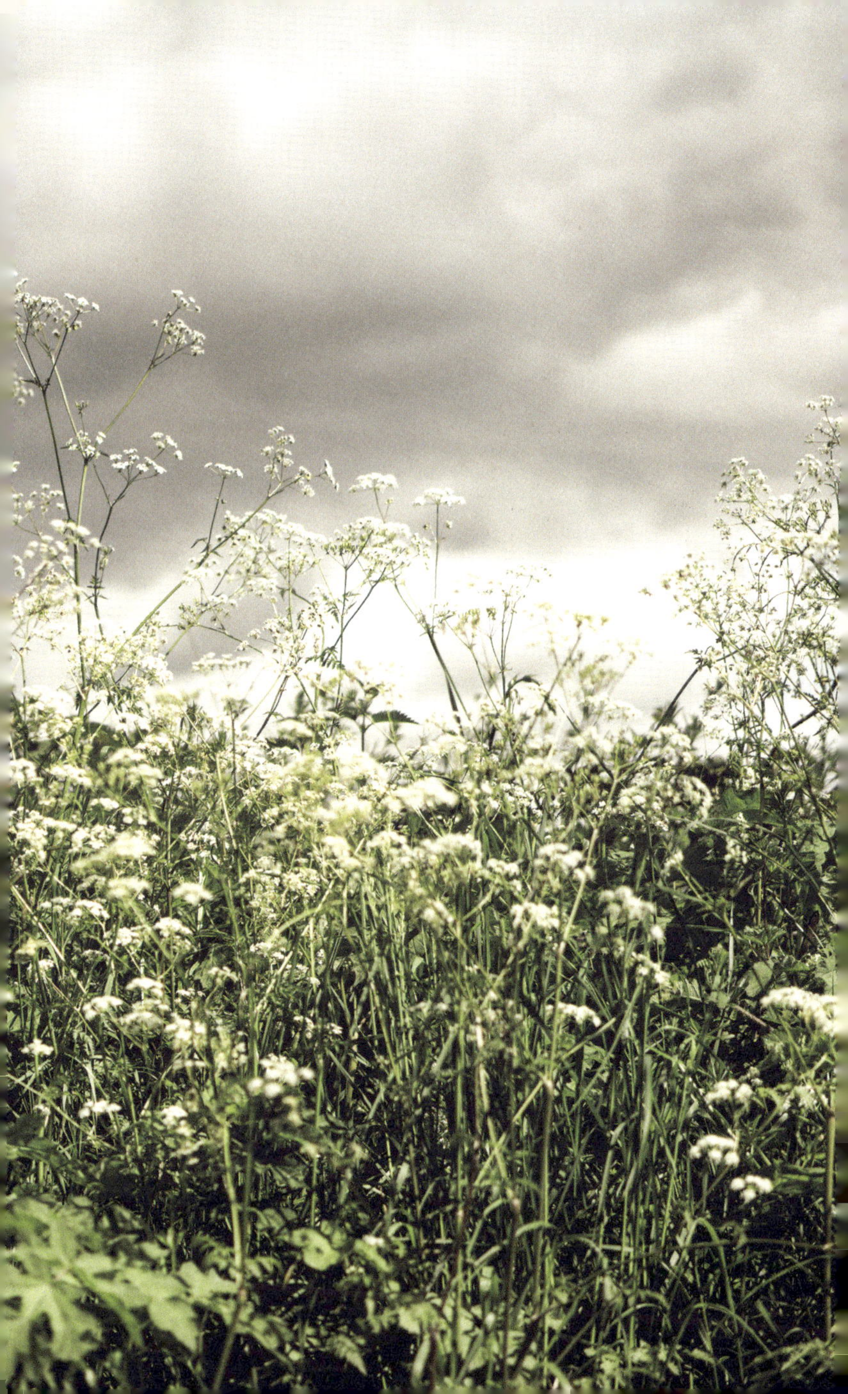

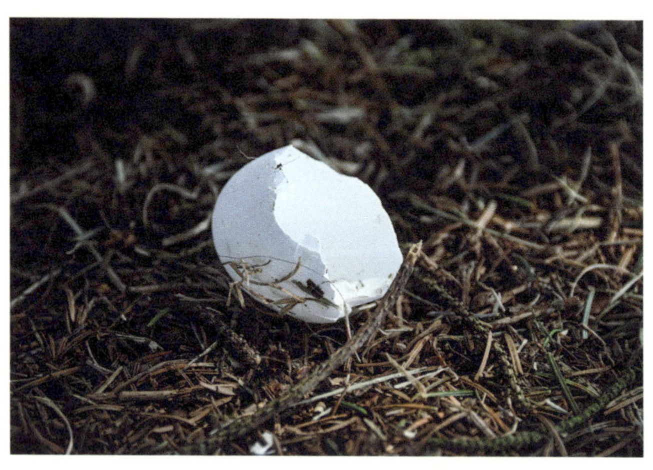

Previous: Ian Potter, *Towards Brightwell Barrow*, 2023
Above: Josie George, 2023

SMALL

It's always the small that
gets you, a wee act
of kindness, the tiniest detail,
a stranger's caress,
your heart, the way you react
when faced with the trials.
The gift of a bluebell, an embrace,
Oh – the yellow gorse,
the crows lined up
from the train window.
Beauty, inches close to sorrow.

— *Jackie Kay*

Practice 1

LOOKING AND LISTENING

I sit by the water's edge and wait. It appears that nothing is happening when I first arrive. That's how impatience expresses itself. If I stay in one spot long enough, the world begins to open.

— Barbara Bash, *True Nature*

Find a quiet spot to sit outdoors and watch whatever is right in front of you for 20 minutes. You needn't seek out anywhere special or new; your garden or a bench in your local park is perfect. This is an exercise in patience and observation, so don't take photographs or write notes; just look and listen. If you feel bored or distracted, notice this, but don't give up.

It's tempting to expect the natural world to perform for us or to treat it as something to be interpreted or extracted from. When we release ourselves from this approach, stilling our mind from some of its habitual jumpiness and judgement, we have a greater chance of noticing what's actually going on. It's a beautiful thing to make art inspired by the natural world, but sometimes just admiring what's there is enough.

Practice 2

GET CLOSE, THEN CLOSER

Pick up something easily available from the land – a leaf, a twig, a piece of fruit or a handful of soil. Use a camera to zoom in as close as you can until its recognisable form falls apart. Notice what happens when you can no longer identify the shapes but find yourself in an abstract realm of colours and patterns.

The smallest object the human eye can see without magnification is about 0.1 millimetres. If we move in closer, we glimpse a wondrous quantum realm where the infinitesimally small seems mysteriously to merge with the unfathomably vast. Although nature provides more than enough observable wonders to keep us nourished for a lifetime, it's worth pondering how much more lies beyond our visible spectrum. You could think of this exercise as a kind of perceptual yoga, a stretch of consciousness that joins the intimate with the ultimate.

Practice 3

GO BAREFOOT

It's all there, waiting for our attention. Take off your shoes, because you are always on holy ground.
— Katherine May, *Enchantment*

Stand barefoot on a patch of the earth. Hard rock, soft sand, sticky mud or mown grass all offer up different sensations. Some of these we have been taught to enjoy, others to recoil from. Try to resist these received opinions and let your feet savour whatever they encounter. Who cares if you get a bit dirty?

Our feet have more nerve endings per centimetre than any other body part, making them acutely sensitive to texture, pressure, temperature and pain. No wonder we usually wear shoes. But a special kind of experience is available when we use these remarkable receptors. Wiggle your toes and enjoy the rubbing, prickling, crumbling, tingling or oozing sensations as you engage skin-to-skin with the ground. Imagine roots descending from the soles of your feet, burrowing deep into the earth and weaving around other underground life-forms. Many people find this exercise helps them feel calmer and more connected to solid ground.

Practice 4

A BUG'S LIFE

It's easy to underestimate insects. They may be small, but they make up the most diverse group of all organisms on Earth. There are around ten quintillion alive at any given time – that's about two billion creepy crawlies for every human.

When did you last give an insect your close attention? Not with the intention of zapping it but admiring its form or flight. Head outdoors, lift a stone and find an earwig. Look in a dusty corner of your house and see if a spider is spinning a web. Next time you find a dead fly, pause before you brush it away and look at its strange and marvellous body.

It may not feel like a challenge to admire a ladybird or a bumblebee but most of us feel less affectionate towards the insects that feast on rotting food, dead animals and faeces. Shifting our perceptions could not be more urgent. Mass use of pesticides has created a global insect apocalypse, but without the pollinators, pest controllers and decomposers, no ecosystem can thrive. See if you can move beyond fear or disgust and become more curious about these surprisingly sophisticated species.

Body

Always there but often ignored, our bodies offer us the most immediate opportunity for everyday wonder. It's easy to feel frustrated when the parts don't work together seamlessly or ashamed when the shapes don't conform to cultural beauty standards, but our bodies are still among the most sophisticated known organisms in the universe. Every day, a dazzling choreography involving millions of proteins, billions of neurons and trillions of cells enables most of us to walk and talk, laugh and cry, play games, have dreams, feel pleasure and endure pain.

Here are poems and photographs that revel in embodiment. They explore the strangeness of hands and feet, ears and hair, skin and bones. They describe the joys of washing and dressing, touching and tending. And they encourage us to be curious about the mechanics of breathing, sweating, digesting, ageing and healing.

Most of us don't love everything about the bodies we inhabit, but the invitation here is to approach them with less judgement and more gentleness. When they feel painful or alien, we can reflect on how strange it is to occupy a physical form that doesn't match our feelings. When they feel capable or aroused, we can celebrate owning such an awesome piece of sensory apparatus.

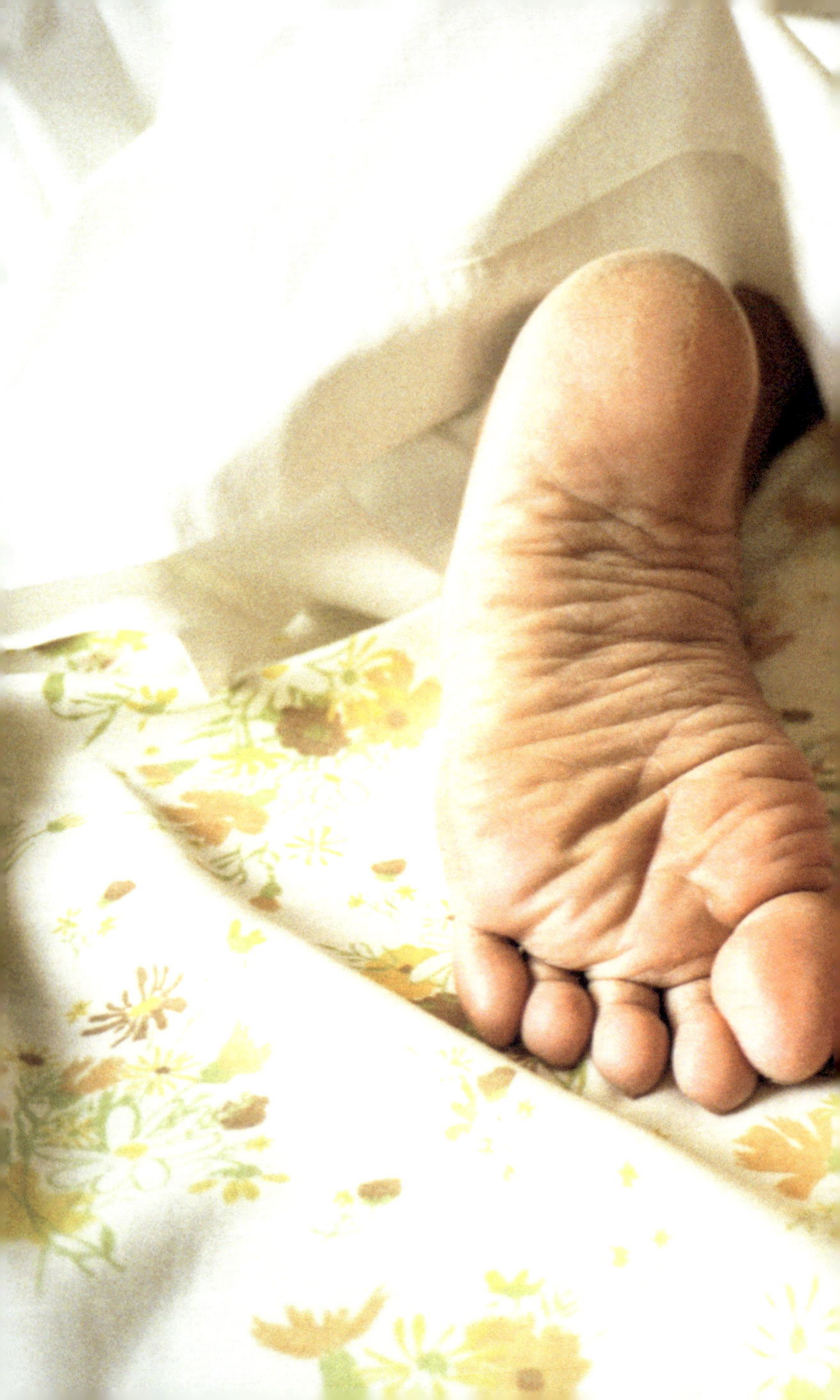

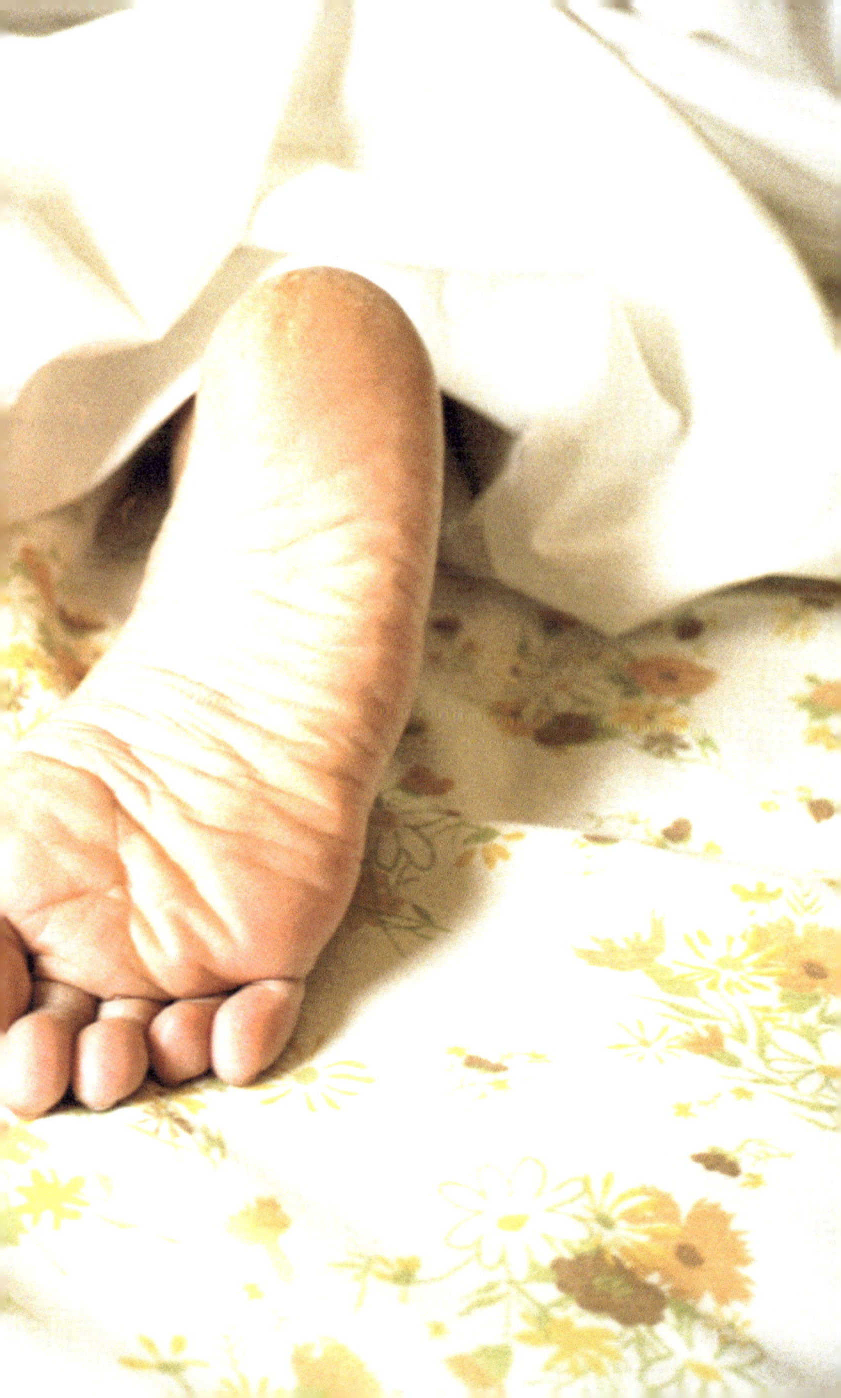

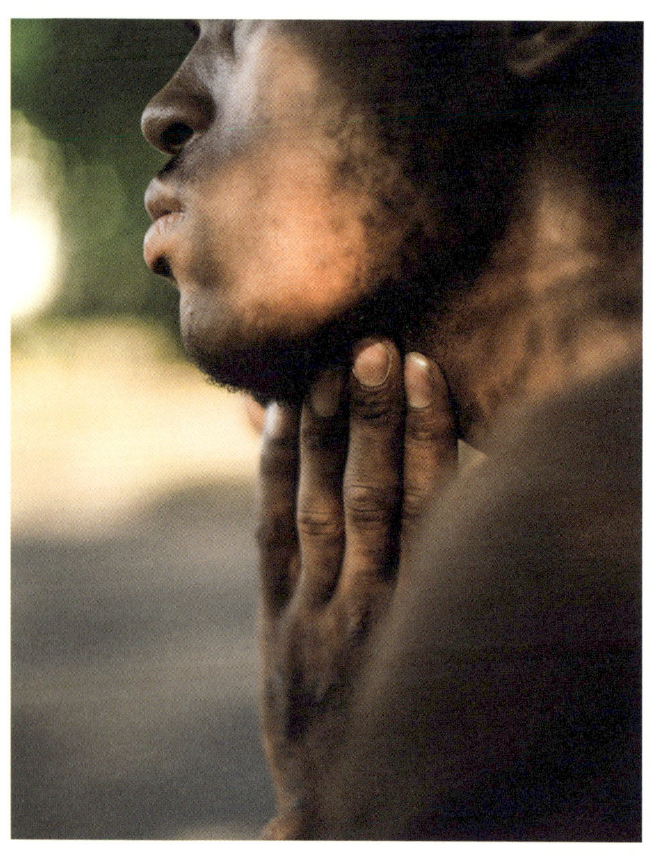

Previous: John Peter Askew, *Feet*
Above: Zora J. Murff and Rana Young, *Untitled*, 2017

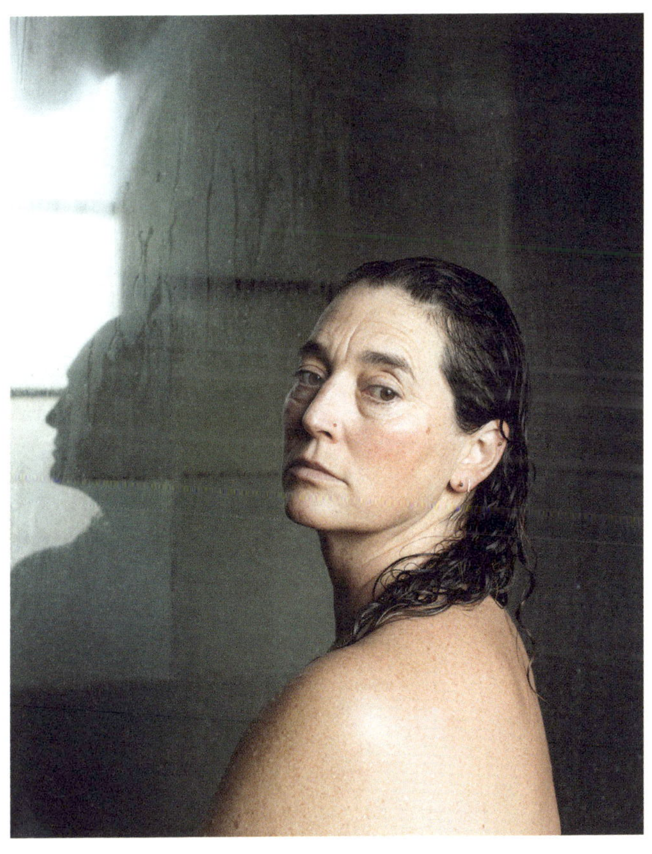

Above: Jenny Lewis, *Self-Portrait, After Gluck*, 2023
Overleaf: Leticia Valverdes, *Lesley*, 2021

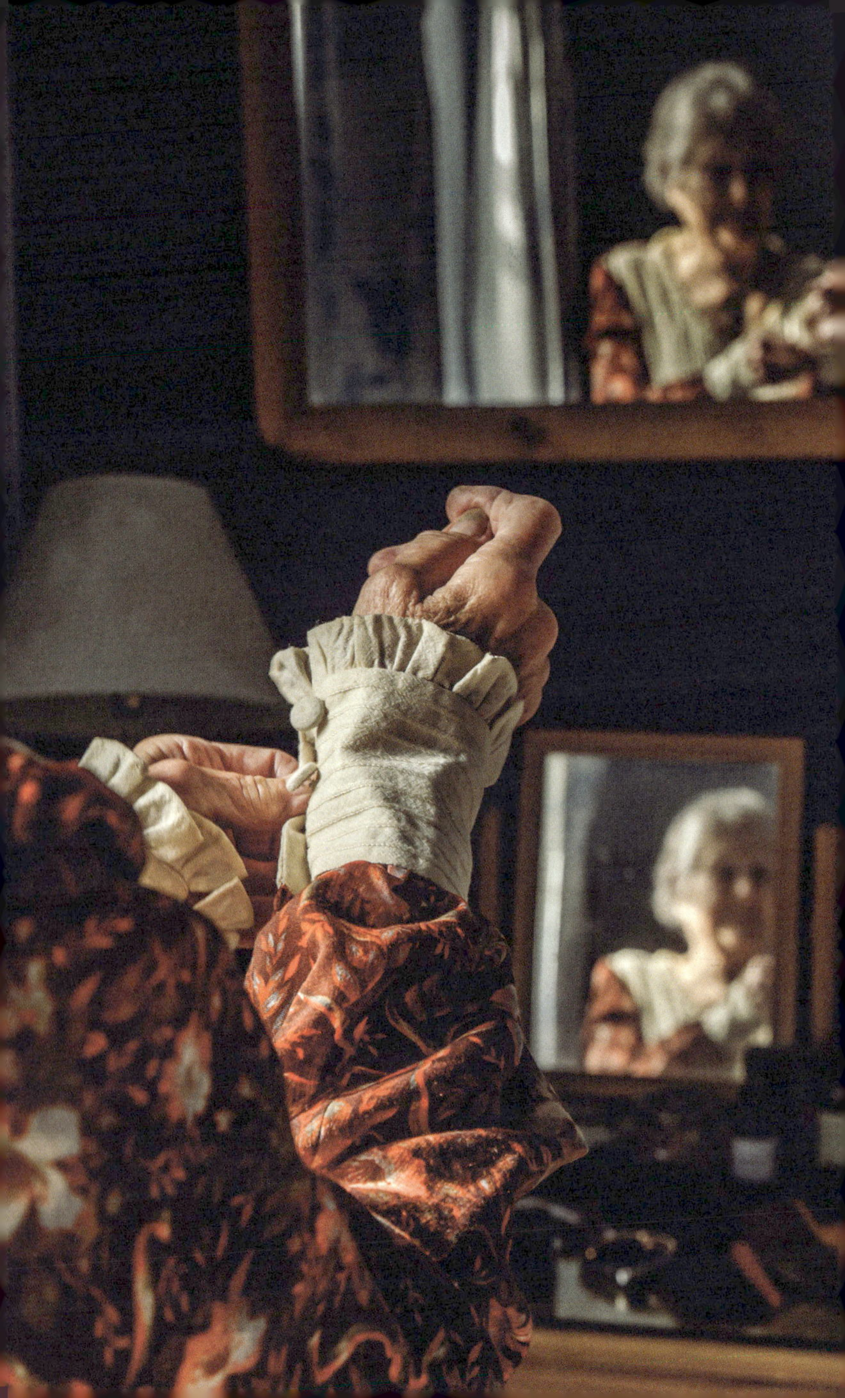

ODE TO BUTTONING AND UNBUTTONING MY SHIRT

No one knew or at least
I didn't know
they knew
what the thin disks
threaded here
on my shirt
might give me
in terms of joy
this is not something to be taken lightly
the gift
of buttoning one's shirt
slowly
top to bottom
or bottom
to top or sometimes
the buttons
will be on the other
side and
I am a woman
that morning
slipping the glass
through its slot
I tread

(continued overleaf)

differently that day
or some of it
anyway
my conversations
are different
and the car bomb slicing the air
and the people in it
for a quarter mile
and the honeybee's
legs furred with pollen
mean another
thing to me
than on the other days
which too have
been drizzled in this
simplest of joys
in this world
of spaceships and subatomic
this and that
two maybe three
times a day
some days
I have the distinct pleasure
of slowly untethering
the one side
from the other
which is like unbuckling

a stack of vertebrae
with delicacy
for I must only use
the tips
of my fingers
with which I will
one day close
my mother's eyes
this is as delicate
as we can be
in this life
practicing
like this
giving the raft of our hands
to the clumsy spider
and blowing soft until she
lifts her damp heft and
crawls off
we practice like this
pushing the seed into the earth
like this first
in the morning
then at night
we practice
sliding the bones home.

— *Ross Gay*

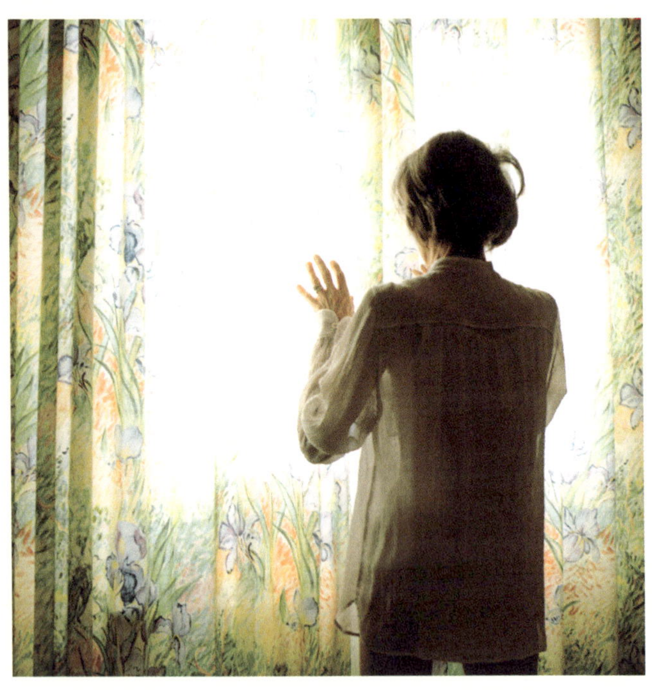

Lydia Goldblatt, *Window*, 2013

HANDS

These hands are wrinkled now.
They clutch
and I wish they wouldn't.
Then I remember
how my first finger learned to point
at what I needed
and then at what I wanted,
how my thumb found my tongue
and soothed the screaming,
how my middle finger stood up that first time
and told my tormentors to fuck off,
how my ring finger offered itself to my happiness,
how my pinky still knows the unshakeable shelter of a promise,
and my palm keeps opening.
It keeps opening.

— *Janeena Sims*

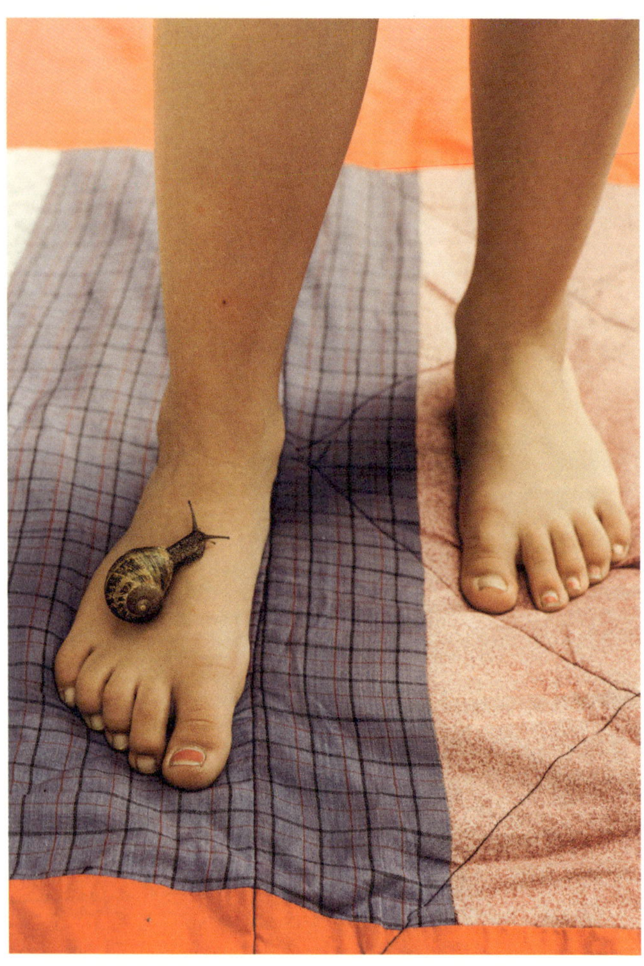

Lisa Sorgini, 2015

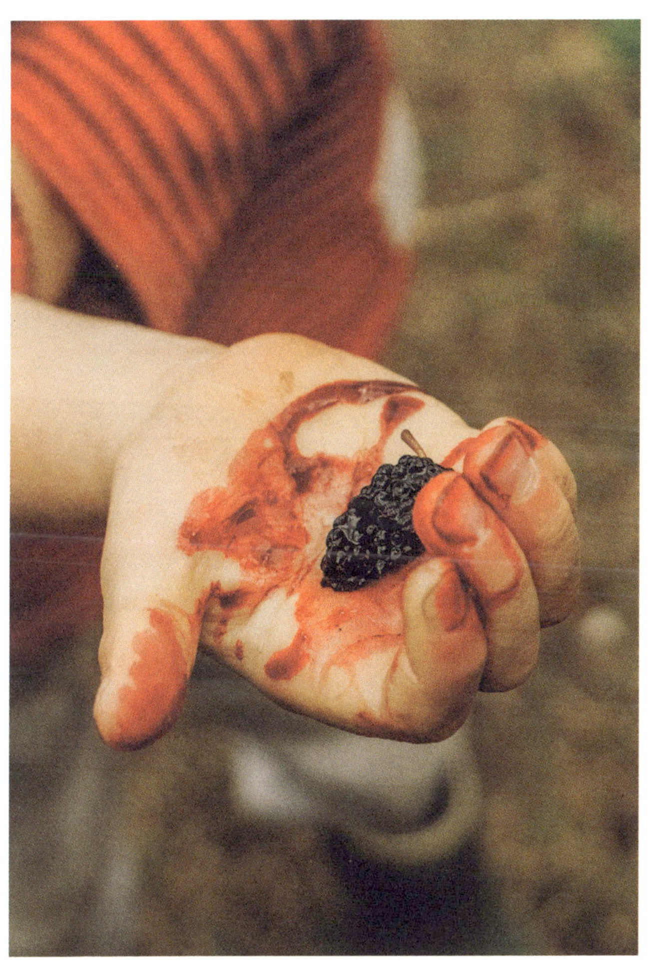

Lisa Sorgini, 2015

SELF PORTRAIT

On the morning of my forty-second birthday

The kneading of my broad swimmer's back by my beloved is the first gift. I nuzzle my pillow and inhale. I sniff my glorious hands. They take their turn at the giving. She says I am a furnace. In the shower I dig into my bestubbled cheeks. I scrape each fingernail against the right bottom corner of my upper left lateral incisor. My marvelous mouth pats the harvested skin into a soft dab. It rests tasteless on my tongue until I step out. My comb tickles my lips with a bouquet of pandemic hair. I sample the bitter end of a Q-tip and am satisfied. The fennel toothpaste searches me and tries me and finds me lacking in a few places. For Jael still sleeping I am a squeeze at their ankle. For Armand I am a known engulfment from behind. For Azel I am a quip and a laugh on his chest. For loafed and purring Angel I am a massive swoon. For hungry Nib I am two legs to rub against back and forth and to loop around with the most eloquently insistent tail in the animal kingdom.

— *John Lee Clark*

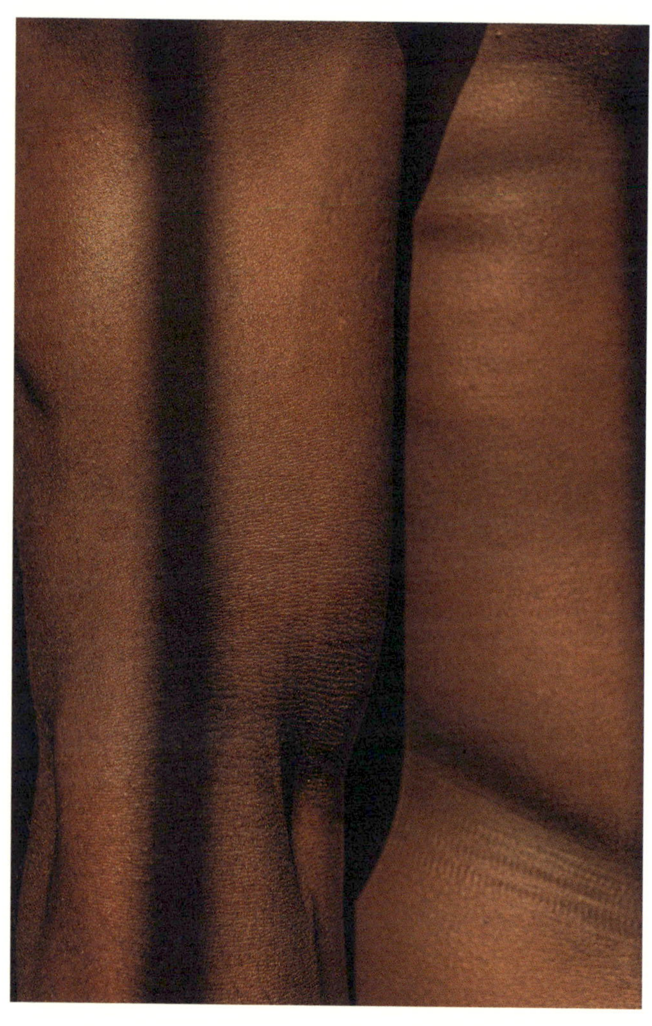

Dylann Hendricks, 2021

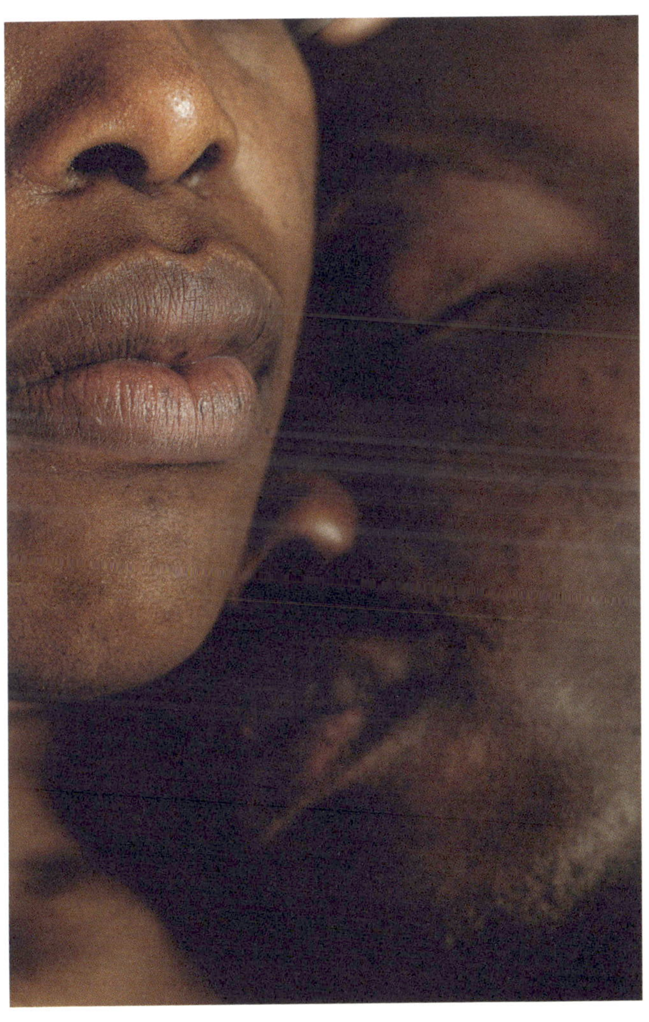

Dylann Hendricks, 2021

Overleaf: Polly Alderton, 2017

SLEEPING WITH YOU

Is there anything more wonderful?
After we have floundered
through our separate pain

we come to this. I bind myself to you,
like otters wrapped in kelp, so the current
will not steal us as we sleep.

Through the night we turn together,
rocked in the shallow surf,
pebbles polished by the sea.

— *Ellen Bass*

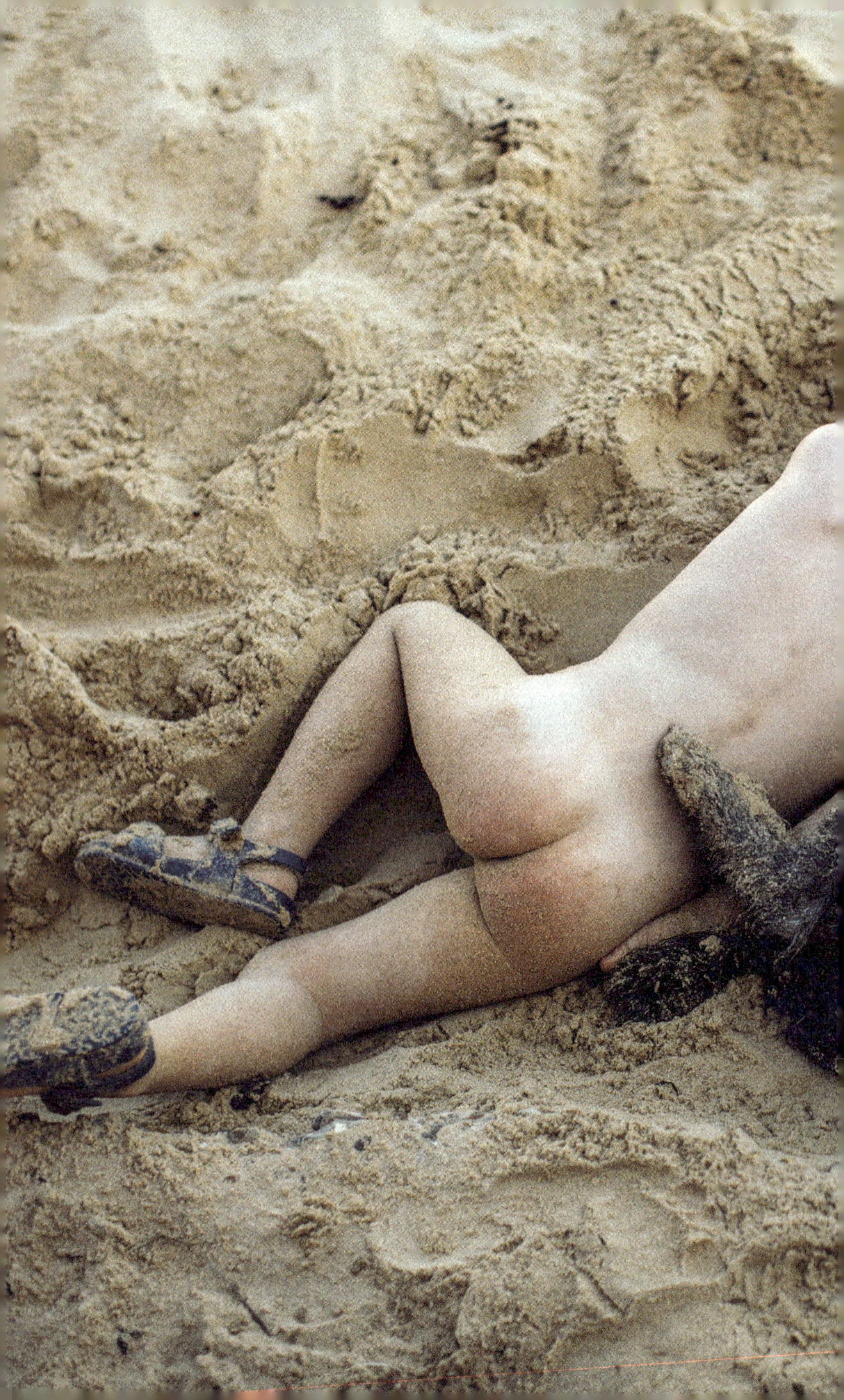

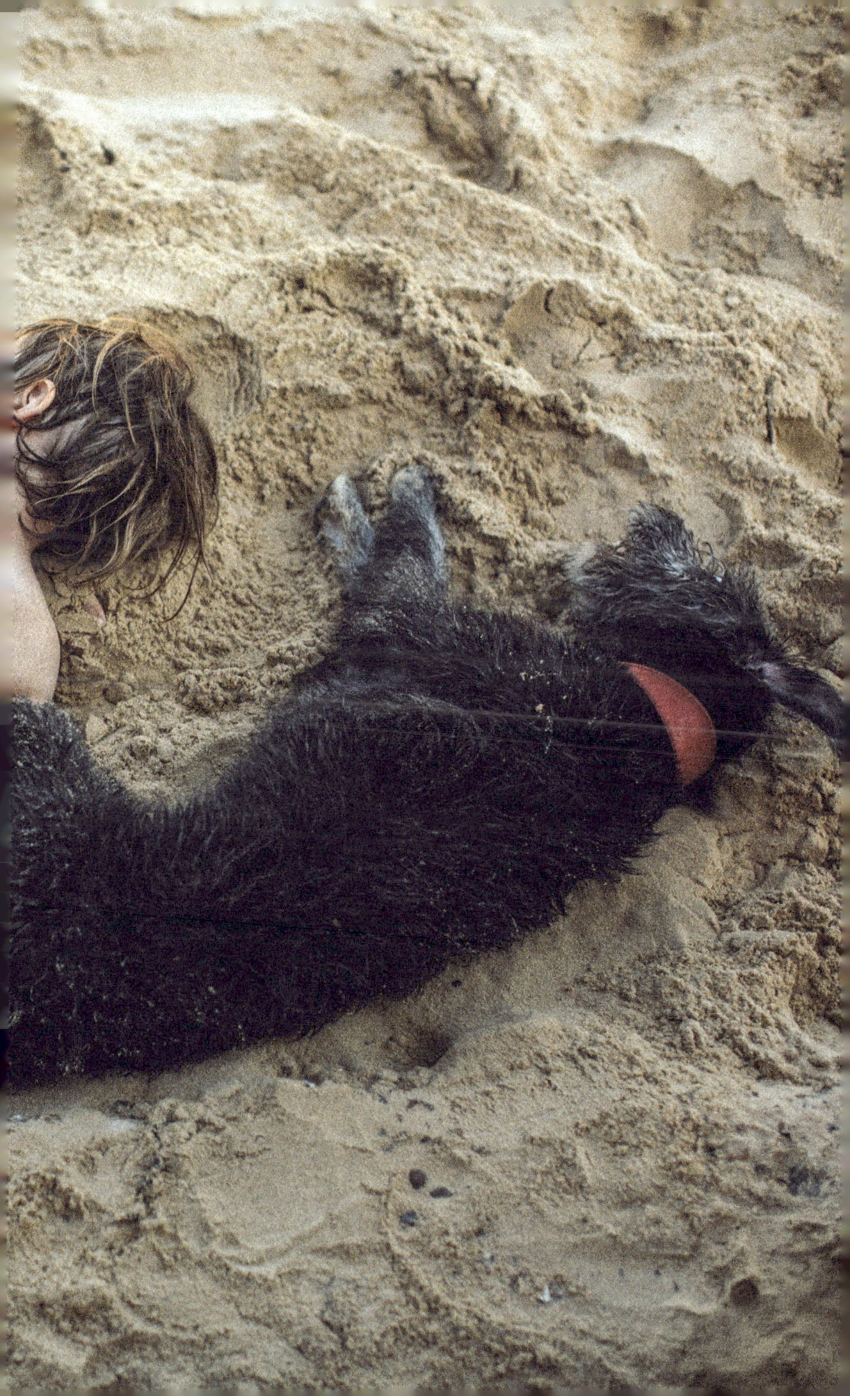

Practice 1

WHAT'S WORKING WELL

Just sitting quietly, doing nothing at all, your brain churns through more information in 30 seconds than the Hubble Space Telescope has processed in 30 years.
— Bill Bryson, *The Body*

Whether we suffer from small aches and pains or experience more severe injuries or sicknesses, many of us tend to focus on what's wrong with our bodies. A question often posed by those treating pain-related stress is, 'What's working well?' It guides us to offer a little more appreciation to all those body parts that are quietly and efficiently doing their job.

Are you breathing as you read this? Then spare a thought for your lungs, which inhale and exhale over 20,000 times a day, enabling all your other organs to function. Can you concentrate on what you are reading? Then ponder the neurotransmitters that facilitate billions of electrical signals to fly around your brain every second. Are you able to sit upright while holding this book? Then consider the hundreds of bones, muscles and nerves working together to prevent you from collapsing. Our bodies work night and day, never asking for any thanks. We needn't let that hold us back from giving them some.

Practice 2

FEELING YOUR WAY

John Lee Clark's 'Self Portrait' (p.105) is a rapturously sensory poem. Lee Clark is deafblind, and his words reveal a heightened capacity to explore and communicate through touch, space and reciprocity. Try reading his poem as a series of instructions on how to savour more of your everyday experiences.

Pay attention to the quality of different fabrics you encounter during the first hour of your day – bedsheets, towels, clothes, shoes, sponges, brushes.

Relish the sensory experience of your morning groom. Rub your tongue over your teeth and around your mouth. Notice the feel of your toothbrush and the taste of your toothpaste. Take a little more time than usual to enjoy the pleasure of tousling, brushing or combing your hair.

Make and eat breakfast using only your hands, smelling them regularly as you do. This might be easier with a piece of fruit than a bowl of cornflakes, but making a mess might not be such a disaster.

Cherish the different experiences of physical connection you have as you encounter members of your household – both humans and pets.

Practice 3

SHOW OF HANDS

The hand is where the mind meets the world.
— Carl Zimmer, *The Common Hand*

Take a close look at your hands. Rub the palms together. Make a fist, then spread the fingers out wide. Touch each fingertip to your thumb and feel how the bones, tendons, muscles and nerves work together to enable incredible dexterity and sensitivity. Each of your hands contains 29 bones, 123 ligaments, 34 muscles, 48 nerves and two main arteries. They are the expression of more than four billion years of evolution.

Now notice how different one hand is from the other, observing the shape of each digit, any scars, marks or moles, rings, tattoos or other forms of ornamentation.

Reflect on some of the things your hands can do: dig, grasp, push, build, cook, write, paint, stroke, fight. What activities do you engage in that stretch the capacity of these extraordinary precision tools? Do you make patisserie, play the piano or bring a healing touch to other bodies?

Try drawing or photographing each one of your hands, noticing what happens when you shift from the dominant to the less dominant one.

Practice 4

HEALING TALES

Consider some of the ways your body is able to repair itself.

Begin by observing any bruises, blisters, swellings or scabs – places where healing processes such as inflammation or blood clotting are now active.

Try to remember previous injuries, pains or strains: rub your hands over old scars, feel any bones that were once broken and notice stretch marks where your skin has adapted to change.

Finally, give some thought to the body's invisible regenerative processes: the way your skin is endlessly renewing itself and how your immune system is constantly fighting off infection. Our bodies typically replace around 25 million damaged, destroyed or dead cells every second.

Of course, our capacity for healing is not only physical but also mental. Most of the time, we can regulate ourselves after feeling upset, stressed or anxious and recover a sense of meaning after painful losses. Consider your experiences of emotional resilience, appreciating your capacity to feel joy even though you have suffered.

Overleaf: Kathryn Martin, *This Sodden Ground*, 2023

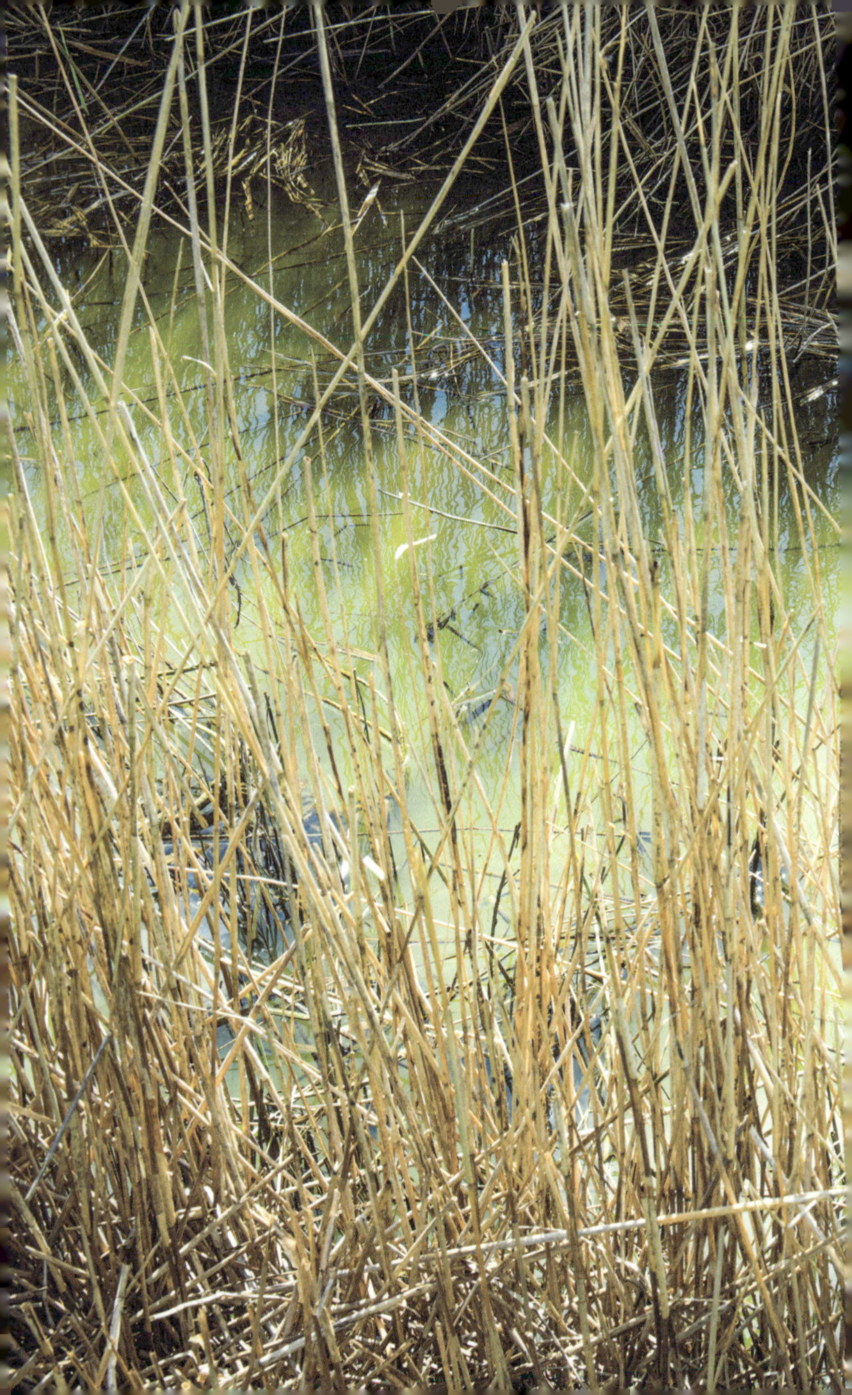

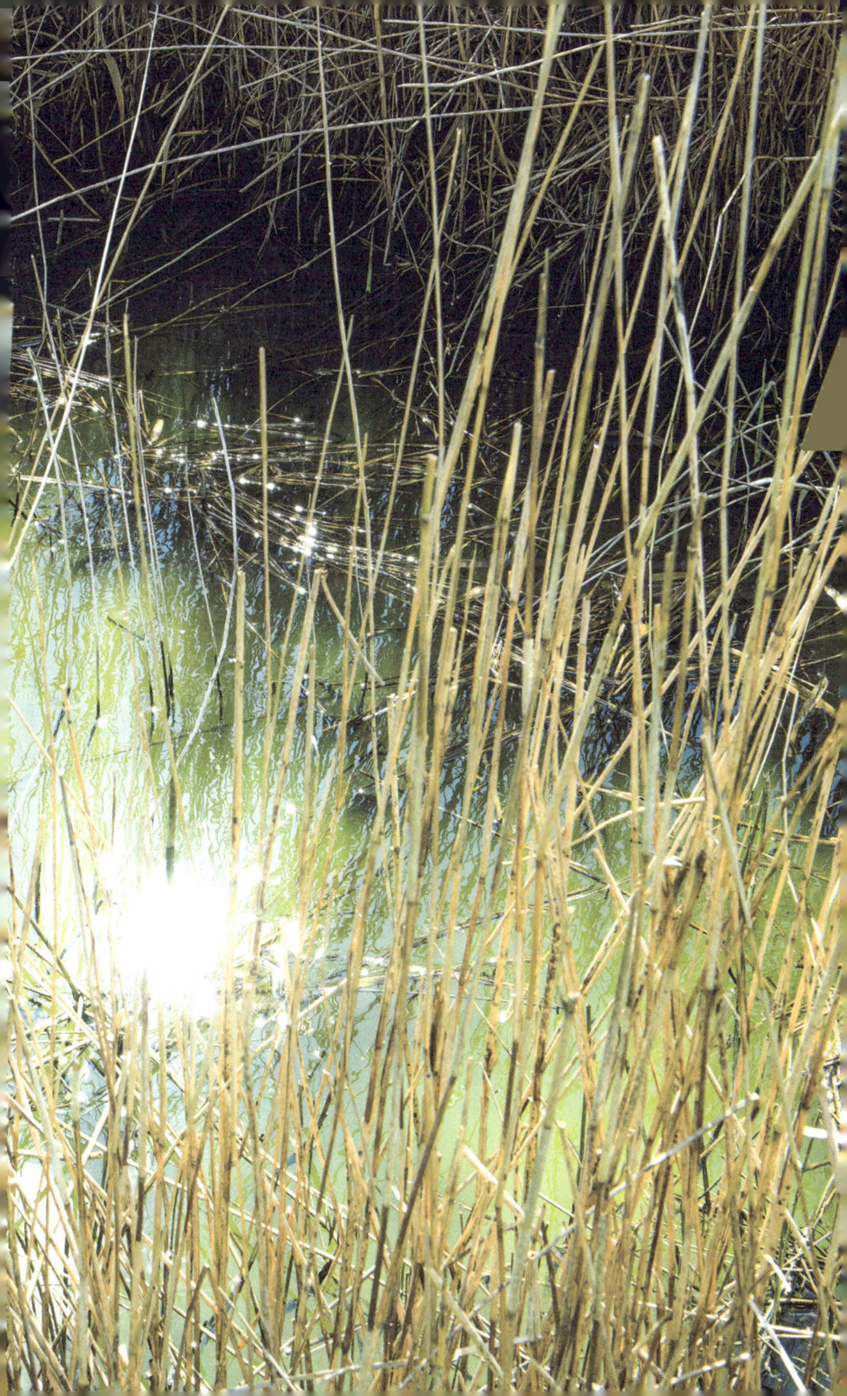

On Not Giving Up

The world is full of painful stories. Sometimes it seems as though there aren't any other kind and yet I found myself thinking how beautiful that glint of water was through the trees.

— Octavia Butler, *Parable of the Sower*

This book is about trying to see the world with fresh eyes, but there are days when it feels hard to shake off a sense of weariness or overwhelm. When we wake up to difficult news, face grim statistics or witness acts of cruelty, the desire to retreat can be a natural response. This may be when the practice of everyday wonder matters most. It isn't about denying or turning away from what's broken or hurting but about putting up some resistance to the drip-feed of painful stories.

The alarming and the divisive will always rise to the surface of public conversation, voices of urgency and doom shouting louder and louder to be heard over one another. But we don't have to amplify what we don't want to intensify.

If the world we long for is one rich in care and compassion, delight and diversity, then it's up to us to seek and magnify these things. Stories of disaster and destruction are plentiful but so are stories of goodness and grace. It's our choice which of these to give our attention to.

With our brains hardwired to focus on dangers, a mental re-orientation towards what is hopeful and uplifting takes determination and practice. We can think of everyday wonder as a kind of spiritual survival muscle, one that grows when we exercise it and shrivels when we don't. As I hope this book has shown, we don't need to cradle a newborn baby or stand on top of a mountain to flex this muscle. We can quietly appreciate a hand gently held or a door generously opened, the first new buds of spring or the last yellow leaves of autumn. Savouring such small delights helps build our immunity against despair. Writer Electra Rhodes puts it succinctly: 'I have to keep reading beautiful things. Listening to beautiful things. Looking at beautiful things. I have to keep thinking about all the beautiful things. Yes, so I am fortified enough to encounter the horror. But for their own sake, too.'

The word 'glimmers' has been used to refer to the micro-moments of joy we can pull from the fabric of our ordinary lives. Attending to glimmers plays an important role in regulating our nervous systems, especially those that have been bent out of shape by repeated exposure to painful emotions. Even on days filled with difficulty, we can usually find small sparks of joy and connection by stroking a pet, smelling our coffee or exchanging a smile with a stranger. As Jackie Kay writes in her poem 'Small' (p.85), beauty is often found 'inches close to sorrow'.

It is all, in the end, a matter of keeping our hearts open. And an open heart is both more available to joy and more vulnerable to sorrow. Such exposure can be unsettling, but it's better than the creeping numbness that is becoming such a common response to the many troubles of the world. In this time of global challenge and catastrophe, there may be nothing that should concern us so much as the closing of hearts.

Instead of adding to the chorus of despair or turning away when it all feels too much, let's keep quietly turning *towards* the world, in its glory and its devastation. Let's savour the wind on our faces, the sun on our floorboards, the dew hanging from a branch or the sweat building on our brow. And let's resist the darkness by shining more light on the many small flickers of goodness and flashes of beauty. They are always there, waiting patiently for our attention.

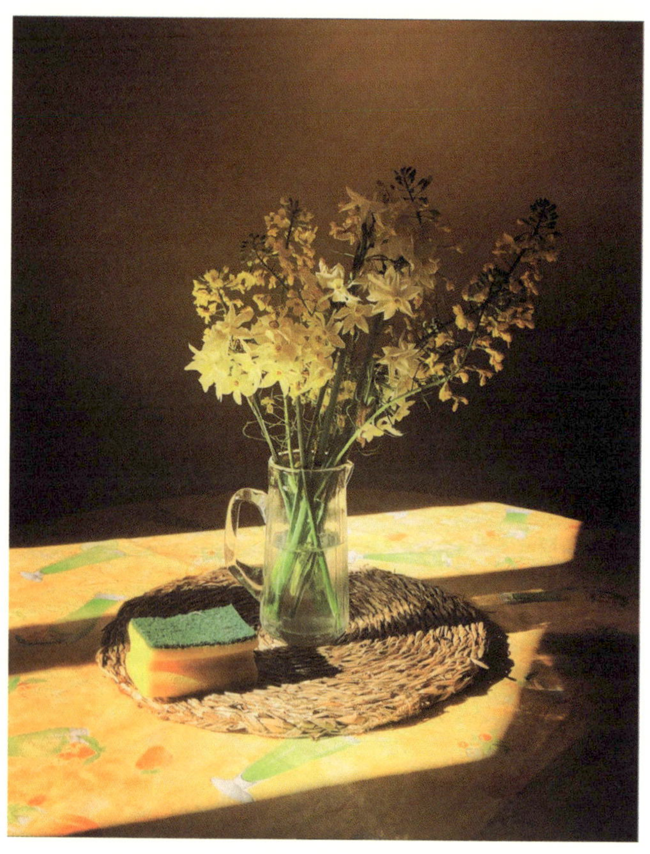

Elizabeth Woolfenden, *Coming To My Senses*, 2024

MORNING AFTER

Again the chance to praise
the same room, the same floor,
the same view, the same tea,
the same image in the same mirror,
which today is startlingly not the same.
Again the chance to find the miracle
in the leaves that fall, the miracle
in the morning sun, the miracle
in the willows beside the pond.
Again, the chance to fall in love
with the same sky, the same field,
the same dirt, the same broken world.
Again, the chance to show up
with these same tired arms
and put them to work,
the same work as yesterday,
which is to learn to lift up,
to heal, to carry, to build,
to be in the world, to praise
the same room, the same floor,
the same view, the same tea.

— *Rosemerry Wahtola Trommer*

IMAGE CREDITS

Cover image: © Alice Oliver, from the series *5p*.

6-7: © Zed Nelson; **16–17:** © Catherine Falls Commercial; **20–21:** © Hiltrud Enders; **24:** © Miquel Llonch; **25:** © Johanna Neurath; **26:** © Celine Marchbank, from the series *A Stranger in my Mother's Kitchen*; **28:** © Nellie Adamyan; **29:** © Jenny Lewis, from the series *UnBecoming*; 30: © Lianhao Qu; **32–33:** © Polly Alderton; **34:** © Anthony Masterson; **37:** © Julia Forsman; **44–45:** © Freya Najade; **48–49:** © Melissa O'Shaughnessy; **50:** © Gil Walker; **51:** © Gil Walker; **52–53:** © Greg White; **56–57:** © Nick Turpin; **60:** © Kathryn Martin; **61:** © Shin Noguchi; **62:** © Jenny Lewis, from the series *UnBecoming*: **70–71:** © Niall McDiarmid; **72:** © Tessa Bunney; **74:** © Robin Friend; **75:** © Colleen Williams; **78–79:** © Kate Kirkwood; **80:** © Freya Najade; **82–83:** © Ian Potter; **84:** © Josie George; **92–93:** © John Peter Askew; **94:** © Zora J. Murff and Rana Young; **95:** © Jenny Lewis, from the series *UnBecoming*; **96:** © Leticia Valverdes; **100:** © Lydia Goldblatt, from the series *Still Here*; **102:** © Lisa Sorgini, from the series *In-Passing*; **103:** © Lisa Sorgini, from the series *In-Passing*; **106:** © Dylann Hendricks; **107:** © Dylann Hendricks; **110–111:** © Polly Alderton; **116–117:** © Kathryn Martin; **122:** © Elizabeth Woolfenden; **126–127:** © Alice Oliver, from the series *5p*.

POETRY CREDITS

9: William Stafford, "You Reading This, Be Ready" from *Ask Me: 100 Essential Poems*. Copyright © 1977, 2014 by William Stafford and the Estate of William Stafford. Re-printed with the permission of The Permissions Company, LLC on behalf of Graywolf Press, graywolfpress.org. **22–23:** Copyright © Craig Arnold, 2009. **27:** "The Teapot" from *Talking into the Ear of a Donkey* by Robert Bly. Copyright © 2011 by Robert Bly. Reprinted by permission of Georges Borchardt, Inc. on behalf of the Estate of Robert Bly. All rights reserved. **31:** Copyright © Zoe Higgins. **35:** From *The Weight of Love* (Negative Capability Press, 2019) by Pat Schneider. Copyright © 2019 by Pat Schneider. Used with the permission of the Estate of Pat Schneider. **47:** "Small Kindnesses" from *Bonfire Opera*, by Danusha Laméris, © 2020. Reprinted by permission of the University of Pittsburgh Press. **55:** Naomi Shahib Nye, "Shoulders" from *Red Suitcase*. Copyright © 1994 by Naomi Shihab Nye. Reprinted with the permission of The Permissions Company, LLC on behalf of BOA Editions Ltd., boae-ditions.org. **59:** Copyright © Carrie Newcomer, 2014. **63:** Reprinted with permission of The Charlotte Seedy Literary Agency as agent for the author. Copyright © 2009, 2017 by Mary Oliver with permission of Bill Reichblum. **72:** Copyright © Josie George. **77:** Patricia Fargnoli, "Reincarnate" from *Hallowed: New and Selected Poems*. Copyright © 2017 by Patricia Fargnoli. Reprinted with the permission of The Permissions Company, LLC on behalf of Tupelo Press, tupelopress.org. **81:** "Stick Season" by James Crews, forthcoming in *Breathing Room: Poems of Rest & Retreat* (Mandala/Earth 2026). Reprinted with permission of the author. **85:** Small by Jackie Kay. Copyright © Jackie Kay, 2017, used by permission of The Wylie Agency (UK) Limited. **97–99:** "Ode to Buttoning and Unbuttoning My Shirt" from *Catalog of Unabashed Gratitude*, by Ross Gay, © 2015. Reprinted by permission of the University of Pittsburgh Press. **101:** Copyright © Janeena Sims. **105:** "Self Portrait", from *HOW TO COMMUNICATE: POEMS* by John Lee Clark. Copyright © 2023 by John Lee Clark. Used by permission of W. W. Norton & Company, Inc. **109:** Ellen Bass, "Sleeping With You" from *Mules of Love*. Copyright © 2002 by Ellen Bass. Reprinted with the permission of The Permissions Company, LLC on behalf of BOA Editions Ltd., boae-ditions.org. **123:** 'Morning After' is printed in *All the Honey* (Samara Press, 2023), and used with permission of the author.

AUTHOR'S THANKS

To all the poets and photographers who have trusted me to share their work here, thank you. To the team at Hoxton Mini Press, who shape every book with such extraordinary care and commitment – thank you. And to my home, my street, the wild places I love and the bodies – both human and animal – that I get to spend my days with – thank you for revealing so much wonder to me. — *SH*

COLOPHON

Everyday Wonder
First edition

Published in 2025 by
Hoxton Mini Press, London

Text by Sophie Howarth
Edited by Florence Ward
Design by Dom Grant &
Francisca Monteiro
Production design by Dom Grant
Proofreading by Zoë Jellicoe

A CIP catalogue record for this book is available from the British Library.

ISBN: 978-1-914314-78-0

Printed and bound by Ozgraf, Poland

Manufacturer: Hoxton Mini Press, 104 Northside Studios, 16-29 Andrews Road, London, E8 4QF, United Kingdom
www.hoxtonminipress.com

Represented by: Authorised Rep Compliance Ltd., Ground Floor, 71 Lower Baggot Street, Dublin, D02 P593, Ireland
www.arccompliance.com

Hoxton Mini Press is an environmentally conscious publisher, committed to offsetting our carbon footprint. This book is 100 per cent carbon compensated, with offset purchased from Stand For Trees.

Every time you order from our website, we plant a tree:
www.hoxtonminipress.com

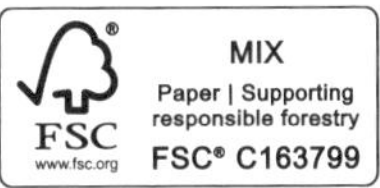

Overleaf: Alice Oliver, 2018

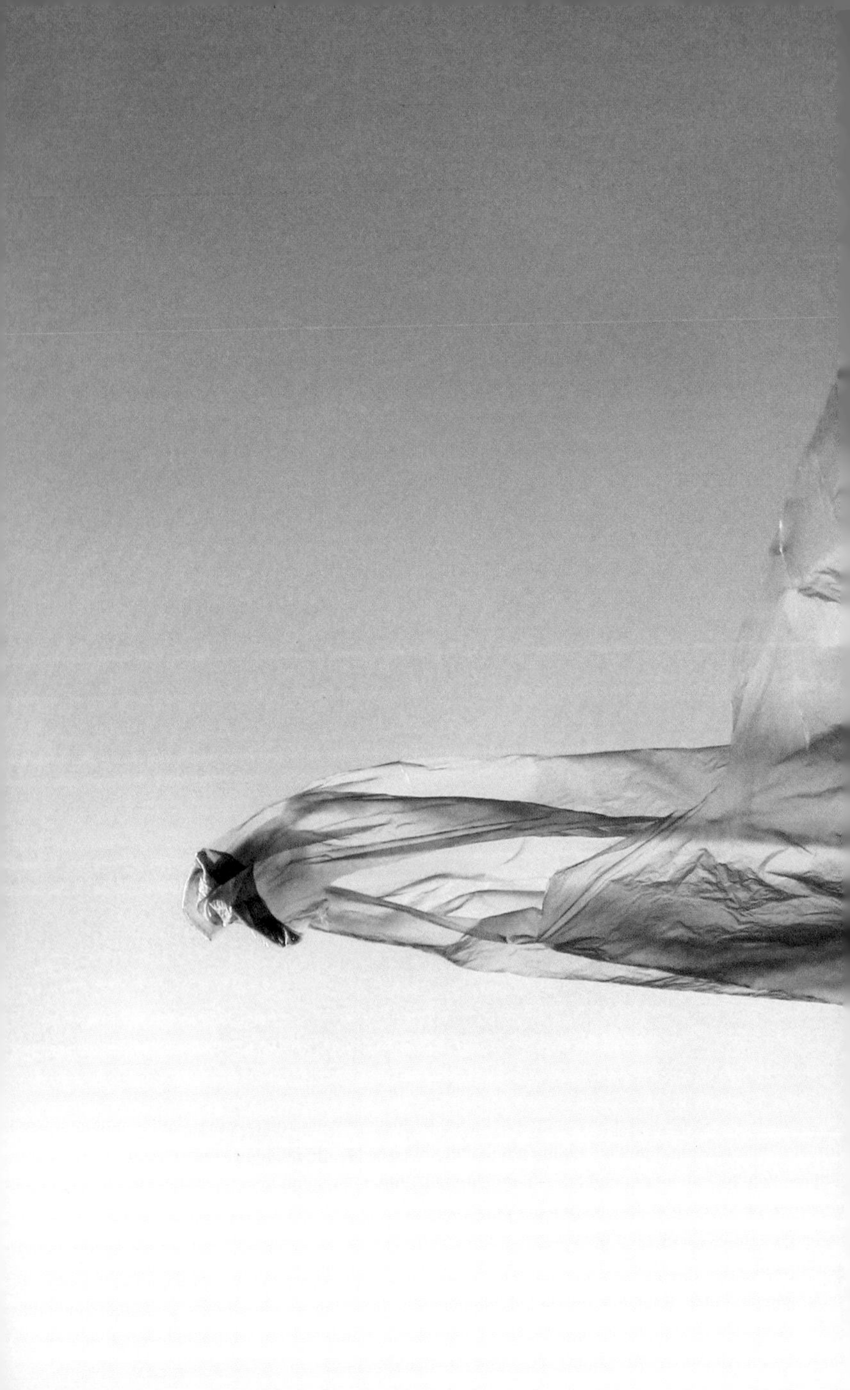

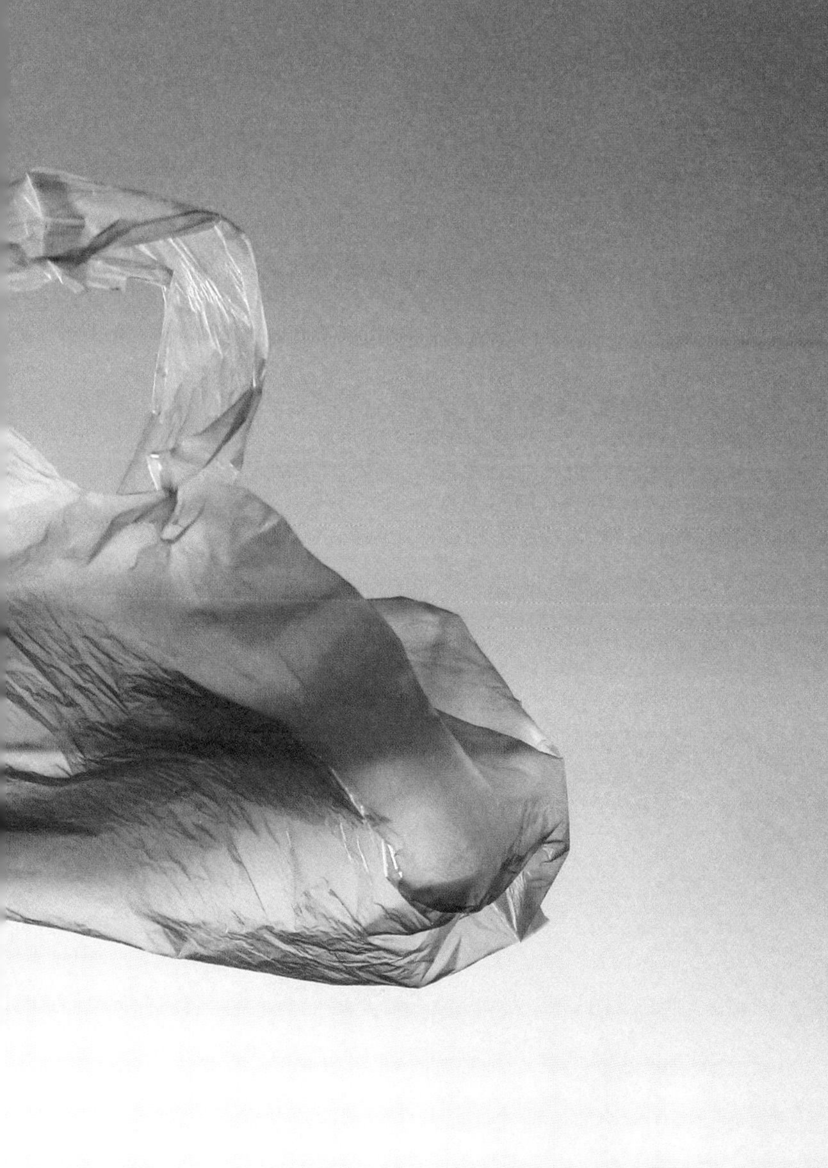

SOPHIE HOWARTH

Sophie Howarth is an artist and activist living in the UK. Her work explores wildness and wonder, justice and joy. Her previous books include *Looking at Trees*, *The Mindful Photographer* and *Street Photography Now*.

HOXTON MINI PRESS

Hoxton Mini Press is a small independent publisher based in east London. We are committed to making beautiful but affordable books that don't screw up the planet. We offset all our printing and we hope that the trees we do use will continue their life as beautiful books that you'll pass on to your grandchildren.